Collins

Cambridge IGCSE™

English

(as an Additional Language)

WORKBOOK

Also for Cambridge IGCSE™ (9–1)

Rebecca Adlard and Tom Ottway

William Collins' dream of knowledge for all began with the publication of his first book in 1819.

A self-educated mill worker, he not only enriched millions of lives, but also founded a flourishing publishing house. Today, staying true to this spirit, Collins books are packed with inspiration, innovation and practical expertise. They place you at the centre of a world of possibility and give you exactly what you need to explore it.

Collins. Freedom to teach.

Published by Collins
An imprint of HarperCollins*Publishers*
The News Building
1 London Bridge Street
London
SE1 9GF

HarperCollins*Publishers*
1st Floor
Watermarque Building
Ringsend Road
Dublin 4
Ireland

Browse the complete Collins catalogue at
www.collins.co.uk

British Library Cataloguing-in-Publication Data.
A catalogue record for this publication is available from the British Library.

Authors: Rebecca Adlard and Tom Ottway
In-house Project Lead: Gillian Bowman
Series Editor: Celia Wigley
Editor: Deborah Friedland
Cover designer: Gordon MacGilp
Production controller: Lyndsey Rogers
Internal designer and typesetter: Ken Vail Graphic Design Ltd
Illustrator: Beehive Illustration Ltd
Printed and Bound in the UK using 100% Renewable Electricity at CPI Group (UK) Ltd

The publishers gratefully acknowledge the permission granted to reproduce the copyright material in this book. Every effort has been made to trace copyright holders and to obtain their permission for the use of copyright material. The publishers will gladly receive any information enabling them to rectify any error or omission at the first opportunity.

Cambridge International copyright material in this publication is reproduced under licence and remains the intellectual property of Cambridge Assessment International Education.

Third-party websites and resources referred to in this publication have not been endorsed by Cambridge Assessment International Education

Acknowledgements: p41 exercise 6e © August_0802/Shutterstock; exercise 8 image 4 © OlegRi/Shutterstock; p55 image 3 © Claudio Divizia/Shutterstock; image 16 © emka74/Shutterstock; p56 bottom left © Oliver Foerstner/Shutterstock; bottom right © Matyas Rehak/Shutterstock; p83 © Andre Roque Almeida/Shutterstock; p91 bottom circle © Deepthought Imagery/Shutterstock. All other images from Shutterstock.

Contents

How to use this book

The *Collins Cambridge IGCSE™ English (as an Additional Language) Workbook* gives you more practice in reading, writing and speaking, as well as in grammar and vocabulary. Each of the main lessons in the Student's Book **(Lessons .1–.5)** has a lesson in the Workbook, so you can study a lesson in the Student's Book and then complete the lesson in the Workbook. Doing the activities in this workbook will give you a deeper understanding of the grammar and vocabulary, as well as improve your spoken and written English. You can do the activities in the Workbook on your own, and they can be done in class or at home for homework. The Workbook provides learning support for the Cambridge IGCSE™ and IGCSE™ (9–1) English (as an Additional Language) syllabuses (0472/0772). We hope that you find this workbook useful.

Answers can be found at www.collins.co.uk/internationalresources

1.1 This is my family

1 Read and match.

| a sister. | b grandma. | c parents. | d mother. | e uncle. |
| f niece. | g cousin. | h grandson. | i nephew. | j aunt. |

1 My mother's mother is my …

2 My grandfather's son is my …

3 My uncle's daughter is my …

4 My mum and dad's daughter is my …

5 My grandma's daughter is my …

6 My mum's sister is my …

7 My mum and dad are my …

8 My aunt and uncle's son is my grandparents' …

9 My sister is my uncle's …

10 My brother is my aunt's …

2 Read and complete David's email with the words in the box.

don't see   has   is   live   'm   're   have

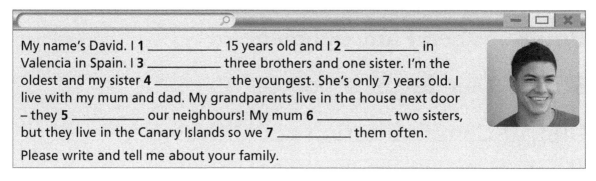

My name's David. I **1** _____ 15 years old and I **2** _____ in Valencia in Spain. I **3** _____ three brothers and one sister. I'm the oldest and my sister **4** _____ the youngest. She's only 7 years old. I live with my mum and dad. My grandparents live in the house next door – they **5** _____ our neighbours! My mum **6** _____ two sisters, but they live in the Canary Islands so we **7** _____ them often.

Please write and tell me about your family.

3 Choose the best option to complete the sentences.

1 My sister is 17 and I am 15. She is *older / younger* than me.

2 I have one *younger / older* brother. He is 9 and I am 16.

3 My birthday is in July. I am *the youngest / the younger* in my class.

4 His bike is *bigger / the bigger* than mine.

4 Write an email to David. Tell him about your family.

1.2 These are my friends

1 Read and complete the crossword with an adjective that describes each person.

1 My little cousin Jack is great! He's always asking questions. He wants to see and touch everything. He's …

2 My big brother does very well at school. He always gets top marks in his exams. He's …

3 I love visiting my grandmother. She's always smiling and laughing. She's never in a bad mood. She's always …

4 I don't like John. He never smiles or says nice things, and he always shouts and throws books across the classroom. He's always …

5 Humberto is my new friend. He comes from Brazil and he tells me all about it: the culture, the cities, the music – everything. I love it! He's very …

6 My granddad doesn't laugh very often. He's …

7 Maria always speaks when the teacher is speaking and she never says please or thank you. She's …

8 In English lessons my partner is called Rebecca. She's nice, but she rarely talks so it's difficult to practise our speaking skills. She's always …

2 Put the words in the correct order to make sentences.

1 called / is / best / Daniel / friend / my _____

2 very / he's / funny _____

3 sad / never / he's _____

4 me / he / happy / makes _____

5 been / for / four / we've / friends / years _____

6 his / I / often / to / go / house _____

7 video games / playing / like / we _____

8 lot / a / talk / we _____

3 Look at the information in the table. Complete the texts using adverbs of frequency.

5	↑	always
4		often
3		usually
2		
1		rarely
0		never

	sad	funny	serious	angry
Ella	1/5	4/5	3/5	0/5
Rachel	0/5	3/5	0/5	1/5
Evan	5/5	0/5	5/5	5/5

Ella's my best friend. I like her because she's __rarely__ sad and she's __never__ angry. She's __often__ funny but she's __usually__ serious too.

My best friend is called Rachel. She's **1** _____ sad and she's **2** _____ angry. She's **3** _____ funny and **4** _____ serious.

I don't really like Evan. He's **5** _____ serious or sad or angry. He doesn't make me laugh because he's **6** _____ funny.

4 Read and underline the correct options.

1 Bill / Bill's often laughs.

2 Javid / Javid's never sad.

3 Olivia / Olivia's always happy.

4 Kieran / Kieran's never remembers my birthday.

5 Li / Li's usually sensible.

5 Write sentences about you using adverbs of frequency and adjectives.

_____

_____

_____

_____

_____

_____

1.3 These are my pets

1 Name pets a–f.

a _____

b _____

c _____

d _____

e _____

f _____

2 Match descriptions 1–5 to five of the pets in activity 1.

1 My pet is long and thin. It doesn't have any legs. It's black and brown. It lives in a glass box. ☐

2 My pet has four legs. It's grey and quite big. It doesn't live in my bedroom. I can ride it. ☐

3 My pet is brown and it has hair on its body and legs. It has eight legs. It lives in a box. ☐

4 My pet is orange and white. His name is Ginger. He has four legs. He lives in the garden and the house. ☐

5 My pet is very pretty. It's yellow and blue. It has two legs. I keep it in a cage in my bedroom. ☐

3 Write a description for the other pet in activity 1.

_____

_____

_____

4 Complete the table.

Personal pronouns	
Subject	**Object**
I	me
you	
he	
she	
it	
we	
they	

5 **Choose the best options to complete the conversation.**

Poppy: Katie, do you have any pets?

Katie: Yes, I do. I have three mice.

Poppy: What colour are **1** *it / they*?

Katie: **2** *Them / They 're* brown.

Poppy: Where do you keep **3** *them / they*?

Katie: In **4** *their / them* cage.

Poppy: Do you clean **5** *themselves / them*?

Katie: No, they clean **6** *them / themselves*.

Poppy: Does **7** *you / your* family like them?

Katie: My mum and dad do, but my brother prefers **8** *his / her* cat.

6 **Read the email and answer the questions.**

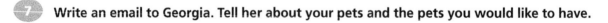

Hi, I'm Georgia. I love animals. I have two horses – a mother and her baby. They're black. They're so pretty. I also have a grey snake called Herbie. He lives in his cage in my bedroom. My mum hates snakes but I think Herbie's cool! We also have a big fat orange cat. Everyone loves her. She's called Molly. I'd like to have a rabbit too, but my dad doesn't like them.

What about you?

1 How many pets does Georgia have? _____

2 What animal is Molly? _____

3 Who doesn't like snakes? _____

4 Which of Georgia's animals are black? _____

5 Which pet isn't thin? _____

6 Why doesn't Georgia have a rabbit? _____

7 **Write an email to Georgia. Tell her about your pets and the pets you would like to have.**

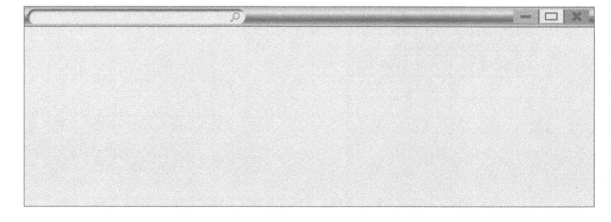

1.4 This is my home

1 Choose a word from the box to add to the words below to make compound nouns.

garden   room   stairs

1 back _____

2 bath _____

3 bed _____

4 dining _____

5 down _____

6 front _____

7 living _____

8 up _____

2 Label the diagram of the house.

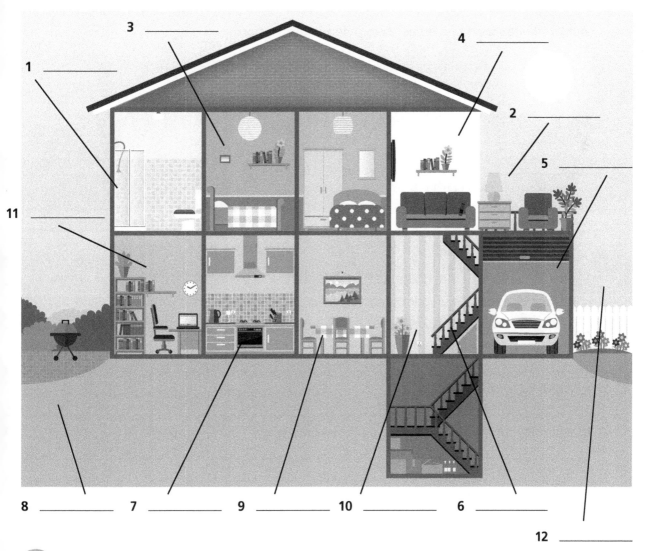

3 _____

4 _____

1 _____

2 _____

5 _____

11 _____

8 _____   7 _____   9 _____   10 _____   6 _____

12 _____

3 Write the words from activity **1** into the correct columns.

Oo	O Oo	Ooo
bathroom		

4 Complete each sentence with *so, and, but* or *because*.

1 Harriet's house doesn't have a back garden, _____ she sits in her front garden.

2 My aunt and uncle have a big house with five bedrooms _____ they have four children.

3 My house has four bedrooms _____ two bathrooms.

4 I don't have a garden _____ I do have a balcony.

5 Ted doesn't have a study _____ his computer and his desk are in his bedroom.

6 My house has an upstairs _____ a downstairs.

7 I don't like the kitchen _____ it doesn't have a window.

8 My friend puts her car in my garage _____ I don't have a car.

5 Look at the floorplan of a home. Complete the description.

This lovely small apartment is on the first
1 _____. Open the front door and you walk into a
nice **2** _____. You then see three doors that open
into the rooms. The apartment has one **3** _____
and a big living room with a nice view through the
4 _____ but it doesn't have a balcony. There isn't
a **5** _____ in the apartment but you can eat at the
table in the living room or in the **6** _____. There
is also a very nice new **7** _____. It's a great place
to live for one person or a husband and wife.

6 Answer the questions about your home. Write full sentences. Practise saying your answers.

1 How many rooms does your home have?

_____

2 How many floors does your home have?

_____

3 Which is the smallest room?

_____

4 Which is your favourite place in your home and why?

_____

_____

5 What colour are the walls in your bedroom?

_____

6 Do you have a garden?

_____

7 Who lives in your home with you?

_____

8 Is there a good view from your bedroom window?

_____

1.5 These are my hobbies

1 Put the hobbies into the correct circles.

climbing cycling the drums football guitar photos running skateboarding yoga

do	play	go	take

2 Look at the information in the table about Ali, Jacob and Sam's hobbies. Answer the questions.

	Monday	Tuesday	Wednesday	Thursday	Friday	Saturday	Sunday
Ali							
Jacob							
Sam							

1 How often does Ali go running? _____

2 How many times a week does Sam do yoga? _____

3 Who does yoga once a week? _____

4 Who doesn't play football? _____

5 When does Sam go running? _____

6 Who never goes skateboarding? _____

7 Who goes cycling most often? _____

8 How often does Jacob go running? _____

3 Read the text and decide if the sentences are true (T) or false (F).

My name's Niall. I'm 15 years old. I don't like sports or drama or art. I don't do any activities after school. I can't play any musical instruments so I'm not in a band. I do like music but I can't sing. I listen to music in my bedroom – my favourite band is WhiteTyger. And I write comics. At the weekends, I work in a supermarket and then I go home. At home I play computer games online with my best friend Hector.

1	Niall doesn't have any hobbies.	T/F
2	Niall plays guitar in a band.	T/F
3	Niall writes stories.	T/F
4	Niall listens to music with his friend Hector.	T/F
5	Niall works in a shop.	T/F
6	Niall plays on the Internet with his friend Hector.	T/F

4 Read the text about Niall again. What are Niall's hobbies?

_____

_____

5 Write answers to the questions. Use complete sentences. Practise saying your answers.

1 What do you like doing in your free time?

_____

2 Choose one hobby. How often do you do this hobby?

_____

3 Do you do this hobby in the week, at the weekends or both?

_____

4 How many hours do you do this hobby for each time you do it?

_____

5 Who do you do this hobby with?

_____

6 Underline the gerund in each sentence.

1 Olga and Nate love dancing.

2 I think swimming in the sea is dangerous.

3 My new hobby is sewing.

4 Doing yoga is a good way to keep healthy.

5 I hate sitting at the back of the classroom.

2.1 At home

Complete the labels under the photos.

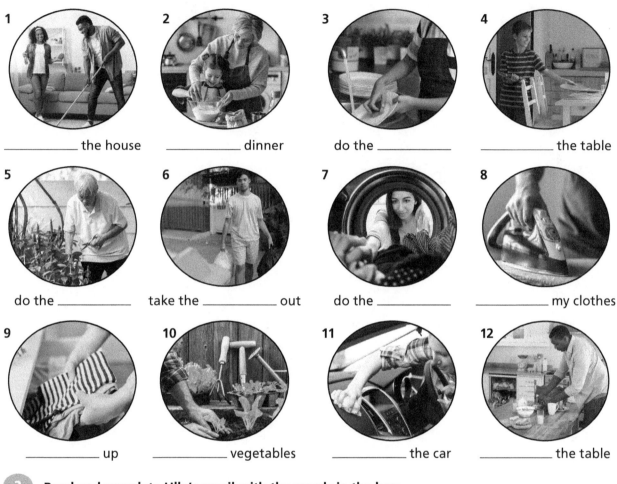

1 _____ the house

2 _____ dinner

3 do the _____

4 _____ the table

5 do the _____

6 take the _____ out

7 do the _____

8 _____ my clothes

9 _____ up

10 _____ vegetables

11 _____ the car

12 _____ the table

2 **Read and complete Ulla's email with the words in the box.**

clean dinner jobs laundry make money rubbish tidy

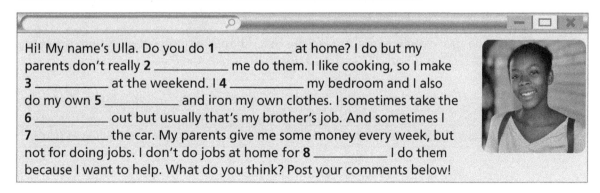

Hi! My name's Ulla. Do you do **1** _____ at home? I do but my parents don't really **2** _____ me do them. I like cooking, so I make **3** _____ at the weekend. I **4** _____ my bedroom and I also do my own **5** _____ and iron my own clothes. I sometimes take the **6** _____ out but usually that's my brother's job. And sometimes I **7** _____ the car. My parents give me some money every week, but not for doing jobs. I don't do jobs at home for **8** _____ I do them because I want to help. What do you think? Post your comments below!

3 **In your notebook, write a post in reply to Ulla. Tell her about the jobs you do at home.**

2.2 At school

1 Write the words for the school subjects.

1

2

3

4

5

_____ _____ _____ _____ _____

6

7

8

9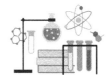

10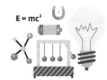

_____ _____ _____ _____ _____

2 Match the present simple and past simple forms of the verbs.

1	is	**a**	had
2	are	**b**	wanted
3	have	**c**	went
4	go	**d**	was
5	like	**e**	did
6	want	**f**	asked
7	do	**g**	took
8	ask	**h**	were
9	take	**i**	liked
10	make	**j**	made

3 3 Look at the past simple verb forms in the box. Choose whether they sound like *made* (/-d/), *asked* (/-t/) or *wanted* (/-ɪd/), and put them under the correct heading.

> decided   enjoyed   liked   lived   needed   picked   shopped   stopped   tried

made (/-d/)	asked (/-t/)	wanted (/-ɪd/)

4 **Complete the sentences with the correct forms of the verbs in brackets.**

1 Today _____ my favourite day of the week because we have music. **(be)**

2 On Mondays, I _____ to my music lesson after school. **(go)**

3 How _____ your maths lesson yesterday? **(be)**

4 _____ you _____ a history lesson yesterday? **(have)**

5 I _____ my homework after dinner yesterday. **(do)**

6 Our teacher _____ us to give a presentation in the lesson today. **(ask)**

7 James _____ three science lessons a week. **(have)**

8 We _____ a drama lesson with Ms Dufort this morning. It was great! **(have)**

5 **Match the questions 1–8 with the correct answers a–h. Practise saying these.**

1 Did you have maths today?

2 Were Pierre and Claude at school yesterday?

3 Where was your biology lesson this morning?

4 Who did you walk to school with?

5 What was your last lesson before lunch?

6 Were you late for art today?

7 Who was your teacher for geography yesterday?

8 Did Raheem do the homework for today's lesson?

a No, he didn't.

b It was Mr Simon.

c It was languages.

d No, they weren't.

e No, I have maths on Tuesday.

f It was in Room 2B.

g I walked to school with Ted.

h No, I wasn't.

6 **Put the words in the correct order to make sentences.**

1 had / physics / a / yesterday / lesson / I

_____

2 lunch / we / English / have / our / break / before

_____

3 school / did / my / I / homework / after / yesterday

_____

4 favourite / class / was / PE / my / yesterday

_____

5 have / did / maths / yesterday / you / ?

_____

6 school / go / did / to / week / last / you / ?

_____

7 **In your notebook, write a paragraph about your best day at school last week.**

● Which subjects did you have?

● Why was it your favourite day?

_____

_____

_____

_____

2.3 At the weekend

1 Look at the pictures that show what Liam does at the weekend. Write the correct letter for each sentence.

a
b
c
d

e
f
g

1 At the weekend, Liam always goes to the gym.

2 On Saturdays and Sundays, he goes for a walk for about two hours.

3 When his friends are doing jobs at home, Liam is relaxing on the sofa.

4 He goes out with his friends on Saturday afternoon.

5 In the summer, he usually has a picnic with his family on Sundays.

6 He sometimes eats out in a restaurant.

7 He likes going to the cinema on Saturdays.

2 Complete the zero conditional sentences with the correct form of the verbs in brackets.

1 If it _____ **(be)** a nice day, I _____ **(go)** to the park.

2 If I _____ **(be)** tired, I _____ **(not get up)** early.

3 When she _____ **(be)** late, she _____ **(run)** to school.

4 When it _____ **(be)** winter, Zack _____ **(not / walk)** to school.

5 When she _____ **(finish)** her homework, Karen _____ **(be)** happy.

6 If we _____ **(have)** some money, we _____ **(go)** to the cinema.

3 Complete the sentences about you.

1 I go to the park _____*if it is a nice day.*_____

2 If I am tired, _____

3 I run to school when _____

4 I don't walk to school when _____

5 I am happy when _____

6 If I have some money, I _____

4 **Read about what three teenagers do at the weekends and answer the questions.**

A

I often meet my friends at the weekend in the park when the weather is nice – not in winter! But this weekend I stayed at home on Saturday and Sunday. I usually go and see my grandmother on Sundays for lunch. But last weekend I didn't. I watched movies at home with my brother.

Sam

B

If I play football on Friday, I don't get up early on Saturday morning, I stay at home and relax. In the evenings, I often cook lunch for my family. But last weekend I didn't. I went with my family for dinner to a restaurant in my city. It was fun.

Kelly

C

I usually get up at about 7.30 on Saturdays and Sundays. I love sports and I play basketball in the park in the morning at 8 o'clock. This weekend, I went to my friend Sally's house on Saturday morning and then in the afternoon I went shopping with my mum.

Joan

1 Who often gets up early at the weekend?

2 Who gets up late on Saturdays after playing sport on Friday?

3 Who didn't see someone in their family at the weekend?

4 Who likes to meet friends in the park when the weather is nice?

5 Who visited a friend on Saturday?

6 Who went to a restaurant last weekend?

5 **Write about what you do at the weekends. Use words from the box and lesson.**
Practise saying this.

get up   meet friend(s)   park   relax   restaurant
Saturday   shopping   sport   Sunday   weekend

_____

_____

_____

_____

_____

_____

_____

_____

2.4 Around town

1 Put the letters in the correct order to make transport words.

1 axit _____

2 mart _____

3 usb _____

4 reryf _____

5 loomtrcecy _____

6 arc _____

7 trome _____

8 otab _____

9 yielccb _____

10 no toof _____

2 Write the transport words from activity 1 that you can see in the photo.

1 _____

2 _____

3 _____

3 Match the questions and answers. Practise saying these.

1 How do you get to school?   a Because it's quicker than the bus.

2 Why do you go by tram?   b No, there isn't.

3 How long does your journey take?   c I take the bus.

4 Can you go to school by bus?   d I went on a train.

5 What transport did you go on yesterday?   e It takes 25 minutes.

6 Is there an underground in your town?   f Yes, I can.

4 Complete the sentences with the prepositions from the box.

> in   in front of   into   off   on

1 Gene got _____ the bus and then walked to the cinema.

2 Sara and Freya were _____ the train.

3 Aya was going _____ town to meet her cousin.

4 Kaleb sat _____ Jay on the tram.

5 Austin left his money _____ the taxi.

5 Complete the story with the past continuous forms of the verbs in brackets.

I **1** _____ (walk) to school when it started to rain, The number 16 tram **2** _____ (come) down the road so I ran to get on it. Then I saw my dad in our car. 'Dad!' I shouted but Dad **3** _____ (listen) to music and he didn't hear me. It **4** _____ (rain) a lot now. People **5** _____ (run) into shops and cafes. I went into a bookshop and I read a book for an hour. The rain stopped. A man next to me in the shop **6** _____ (put) books in his bag. When the police came, they asked me some questions. When I got to school, it was lunch time!

6 Use the words to write sentences with past continuous + *when* + past simple.

1 Helen / read / in her bedroom / when / the cat / jump / on her book.
  Helen was reading in her bedroom when the cat jumped on her book.

2 Emiko / play the guitar / when / her brother / come / into the room.
  _____

3 Henry and Max / walk / in the park / when / it start / to rain.
  _____

4 I / ride my bike / to school / when / I see / my friend Amy.
  _____

5 We / play / football / in the garden / when / the ball / break / the window.
  _____

7 Write a paragraph about transport where you live.

Write about:

● What transport there is or isn't in your town.
● What your favourite form of transport is to get around your town and why.
● How often you use this form of transport and where you go.
● How long your journeys take.

_____
_____
_____
_____
_____
_____
_____
_____

2.5 My time

1 **Complete the sentences with a word from the box.**

> first   last   late   midday   midnight   next   tomorrow   week

1 Monday is the _____ day of the week.
2 Sunday is the _____ day of the week.
3 The _____ day after Sunday is Monday.
4 If today is Tuesday, _____ is Wednesday.
5 When it is 12.00 in the middle of the day, it is _____.
6 When it is one minute after 11.59 pm at night it is _____.
7 There are seven days in a _____.
8 If the bus is _____, I go to school by car.

2 **Today is the 3rd of January. Write the dates or months.**

1 Last month was _____.
2 Yesterday was the _____.
3 Tomorrow is the _____.
4 Next Wednesday is the _____.
5 Next month is _____.
6 The second Friday in January is the _____.
7 The last Saturday in January is the _____.
8 The last day of January is the _____.

3 **Complete each sentence with *at, on in* or *takes*.**

1 Football club starts _____ midday.
2 My journey to school _____ 20 minutes.
3 Our maths test is _____ the 12th of February.
4 My birthday is _____ September.
5 The party finished _____ midnight.
6 Mum has dinner with her friends _____ the last Saturday in every month.
7 School starts _____ 8.45 am.
8 The bus journey to Glasgow _____ three hours.

January

01

M	T	W	T	F	S	S
			1	2	③
4	5	6	7	8	9	10
11	12	13	14	15	16	17
18	19	20	21	22	23	24
25	26	27	28	29	30	31

4 **Match the sentence halves.**

1 It's Otto's birthday party on   a tomorrow
2 Rose has her first driving lesson   b Saturday night.
3 The school holidays   c is at 10 o'clock on Monday.
4 My next piano lesson   d start in July.

5 **Complete the questions for the answers about Lucy's weekend.**

I had a really busy weekend. On Friday night, I played tennis with my brother at the park. Then at 8 p.m. we ate pizza in a cafe near the park. It was delicious. Then we went home and we watched TV.

Then on Saturday morning I went shopping with my friends. I bought some clothes and a new pen for school. Sunday was also busy. I woke up early and did my homework. Then my family had a really nice breakfast outside. It was sunny and warm. Then I went for a run in the afternoon. In the evening I relaxed and watched a film.

1 <u>What did Lucy do on Friday night?</u> ?

She played tennis with her brother.

2 <u>What</u> ?

They went for a pizza.

3 <u>What</u> ?

They went home and watched TV.

4 <u>What</u> ?

She went shopping with her friends.

5 <u>What</u> ?

Some clothes and a new pen for school.

6 <u>When</u> ?

Early.

7 <u>Where</u> ?

In the garden.

8 <u>What</u> ?

She went for a run.

6 **Look at this sentence from the text in activity 5. Practise saying it. Remember to make the underlined syllables sound stronger.**

Then I <u>went</u> for a <u>run</u> in the <u>after</u>noon.

7 **Answer the questions about you. Write complete sentences.**

1 Where did you go yesterday?

_____

2 Who did you see last week?

_____

3 When is your next school holiday?

_____

4 When did you last have an English lesson?

_____

5 When is your next science lesson?

_____

6 What fun thing did you do last month?

_____

3 My life

3.1 Shopping for food

1 Choose and write the names of the fruits and vegetables.

apple banana carrot coconut cucumber
pepper mango onion orange tomato

1 A _____ is a fruit. It's long and yellow.

2 A _____ is orange. You can eat it cooked or fresh in salads. It's a vegetable.

3 A _____ is a hard fruit. It's brown on the outside and white on the inside. You can drink the juice.

4 A _____ is a long green vegetable. You usually eat it cold in salads.

5 A _____ is green on the outside and orange on the inside. You eat the inside part and it's very sweet.

2 Circle the different type of food or drink in each row.

1 burger beef rice chicken

3 sweets cola biscuits eggs

2 pasta cake bread biscuits

4 carrots yoghurt onions tomatoes

3 Complete the sentences with the correct word.

1 Can I have *some* / *any* tea, please?

2 Is there *any* / *many* milk?

3 Would you like *a* / *any* biscuit?

4 I'd like *any* / *some* orange juice.

5 *Are* / *Is* there any potatoes?

6 There *isn't* / *aren't* any sparkling water.

7 Sorry, there *isn't* / *aren't* any eggs.

8 Can I have *some* / *a* large pizza, please?

4 Complete the sentences using *and*, *but* or *or*.

1 I like sweets _____ I don't like cake.

2 I like beef _____ I prefer chicken.

3 I love this salad. It's got tomatoes, peppers _____ carrots.

4 I don't like many fruits. I don't like mangoes, oranges _____ apples.

5 Complete the sentences with the words from the box.

enough kilo many much some

1 Grandpa and Grandma are coming for dinner tonight. Do we have _____ food for seven people?

2 'What do you have for lunch, Fatma?' 'I have _____ pizza and a banana.'

3 I'd like a _____ of tomatoes, please.

4 How _____ apples do you want for the fruit salad?

5 How _____ rice is there in the bag?

6 Order the conversation.

- ☐ How many cakes would you like?
- ☐ No, thank you.
- ☐ Hello, I'd like some cakes, please.
- ☐ Here you are. Anything else?
- ☐ Good afternoon. What would you like?
- ☐ Twelve little cakes, please.

7 Complete the conversations with the correct words and phrases. Practise saying these.

Here you are.	How much
Is that enough	many
No, thank you.	six euros
two litres	What would you like

A

Good morning. **1** _____?

I'd like a loaf of bread, please.

White or brown?

White, please.

Anything else?

2 _____

B

Can I have some beef?

Yes. **3** _____ would you like?

I'd like one kilo, please.

C

Hi! Is there any ice cream?

Yes, there is.

Great! I'd like **4** _____, please.

Chocolate, strawberry or mango?

Can I have one litre of chocolate and one litre of strawberry.

5 _____.

How much is that?

That's **6** _____, please.

D

Hello. Can I help you?

Yes, I'd like some apples, please.

OK. How **7** _____ would you like?
There are six in a bag. **8** _____?

Yes, thank you.

3.2 Eating out

1 Match the questions and answers. Practise saying these.

1 Would you like a starter?

2 Would you like a drink?

3 Would you like a dessert?

4 What would you like for your main course?

a Yes. I'd like the vegetable soup, please.

b No, thanks but I'd like a coffee, please.

c I'd like the chicken and potatoes, please.

d I'd like a mango juice, please.

2 Put the conversations in the correct order. Practise saying these.

Conversation 1

☐ **Customer:** Vegetables, please.

1 **Waiter:** Good evening. What would you like?

☐ **Waiter:** Of course. And what would you like for your main course?

☐ **Customer:** For my starter, could I have the tomato soup, please?

☐ **Waiter:** Would you like vegetables or a salad with your fish?

☐ **Customer:** I'd like the fish, please.

Conversation 2

☐ **Customer:** I don't like ice cream, and I don't want fruit. So, banana cake, please.

☐ **Waiter:** There's banana cake, ice cream or fresh fruit salad.

☐ **Customer:** Yes, please. What is there?

1 **Waiter:** Would you like a dessert?

☐ **Customer:** Yes, please. I'd like tea with cold milk.

☐ **Waiter:** Of course. Would you like anything to drink?

3 Complete the menu for your favourite restaurant meal. Then write a conversation between you and the waiter. Practise saying this.

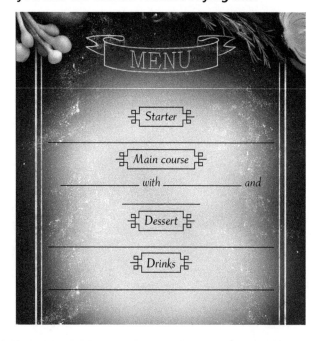

MENU

Starter

_____

Main course

_____ with _____ and

_____

Dessert

_____

Drinks

_____

Waiter: _____

You: _____

Waiter: _____

You: _____

Waiter: _____

You: _____

_____

_____

_____

_____

_____

_____

_____

3.3 Shopping for clothes

1 Put the letters in the correct order to make words for clothes and accessories.

1 redss　　　＿＿＿＿＿＿

2 riskt　　　＿＿＿＿＿＿

3 glansesuses　＿＿＿＿＿＿

4 torshs　　　＿＿＿＿＿＿

5 cajtek　　　＿＿＿＿＿＿

6 esosh　　　＿＿＿＿＿＿

7 surestor　　＿＿＿＿＿＿

8 inertsar　　＿＿＿＿＿＿

9 letb　　　　＿＿＿＿＿＿

10 agb　　　　＿＿＿＿＿＿

11 grin　　　　＿＿＿＿＿＿

12 senrargi　　＿＿＿＿＿＿

2 Complete the table with the words from the box.

bag belt coat dress earrings gold jeans leather necklace
plastic ring sandals shirt silver socks sunglasses trousers

Clothes	Material	Accessory
		bag

3 Match the questions and answers in the clothes shop. Practise saying these.

1 Do you have any shoes?　　　　**a** Yes, they're perfect.

2 Can I help you?　　　　　　　**b** Yes, I'm looking for a new shirt.

3 Can I try on these trousers?　　**c** Yes, we have trainers and sandals.

4 Do they fit?　　　　　　　　**d** I'm a size 30.

5 What size are you?　　　　　**e** Yes, the changing room is next to the lift.

4 Complete the sentences with the correct form of the verb.

1 I hate *try on / trying on* clothes.

2 I often *buying / buy* clothes online.

3 I love *shopping / shop* for old clothes.

4 I prefer *trying on / tried on* shoes before I buy them.

5 I often *buy / buying* books online.

6 I like *going / go* to the shopping centre.

7 I enjoy to *look / looking* at clothes in the shops.

8 I don't want *buying / to buy* any new clothes.

5 Read the sentences. Decide if the <u>underlined</u> words are gerunds (G) or verbs in the present continuous (PC).

1 I hate <u>shopping</u> with my mum.

2 I'<u>m shopping</u> with my mum.

3 <u>Buying</u> clothes online is boring!

4 Kim'<u>s buying</u> a present for her cousin at the bookshop.

5 Li and Amy <u>are trying on</u> trainers in the shoe shop.

6 'Online shopping is better than shopping in stores.'
Do you agree or disagree? Write a paragraph and give your opinion. Practise saying what you have written.

I think online shopping is / isn't better than shopping in stores because …

_____
_____
_____
_____
_____
_____
_____

3.4 Going out with friends

1   **Which place is each person talking about?**

1   Mei: 'Let's go swimming in the sea.' _____

2   Gilly: 'What time does the film start?' _____

3   Saeed: 'The players are wearing red shirts.' _____

4   Lucy: 'Do you want some cake with your coffee?' _____

5   Munir: 'I've just bought a lovely red coat.' _____

6   Basil: 'Do you want to see the monkeys?' _____

7   Luan: 'Let's do some running and then some cycling.' _____

2   **Complete the phrases with the words from the box. Practise saying these.**

> do   how   inviting   let's   love   see   shame   sorry   why   would

1   Thanks for _____ me!

2   What a _____! I can't come.

3   _____ you like to come swimming with me?

4   _____ you want to go to the theatre this weekend?

5   _____ do it another day.

6   I'd _____ to.

7   _____ you later.

8   _____ don't we meet at 8.00?

9   _____ nice!

10   _____, but I can't.

3   **Complete the sentences using *going to* to talk about plans.**

1   Tomorrow, I _____ (go) to the gym with Mica.

2   After school, I _____ (meet) Elisa at the shopping centre.

3   In the morning, I _____ (get up) early at 6.00 and I _____ (go) running with my Dad.

4   Mum and Dad _____ (drive) to Spain next week.

5   After the film, we _____ (get) the tram home.

6   Theo _____ (bring) some biscuits to school tomorrow.

4 Your English friend, Andrea sends you this text message. Choose the photo A–C that shows the place Andrea invites you to.

Hi,

Thanks for inviting me to watch the football match with you tonight, but I can't. I'm going to go to my cousin's house for dinner. Would you like to come to the cinema with me on Saturday? The film starts at 7 pm.

Andrea

A

B

C

5 Write a reply to Andrea's invitation.

- Accept the invitation.
- Suggest where and when to meet.

_____

_____

_____

_____

_____

6 Write another reply to Andrea's invitation.

- Say sorry and refuse the invitation.
- Explain why you can't come.
- Make a suggestion to do something else.

_____

_____

_____

_____

_____

_____

3.5 Going online

1 Choose the correct option to complete each phrase.

1 download **music / online**　　　　　　**2** watch **videos / blogs**

3 take **selfies / group chats**　　　　　　**4** listen to the **radio / tablet**

5 switch on the **website / computer**　　**6** post **online / games**

2 Complete the crossword.

Clues

Across →

3 I … films onto my tablet and watch them on train to school.

6 The app shows that Sara is …, but she hasn't read the message I sent her yet.

7 My friends and I take … with our pets and post them online.

10 I love my … . I take it in my bag every day. I use it to speak to my friends, send messages, listen to music, take selfies, play games and so many other things.

Down ←

1 We have a … in the kitchen. We listen to music on it, but we can't download music with it.

2 My mum writes a … called the *Kitchen Garden*. It's about the vegetables she grows and the meals she cooks.

4 I've just found a really good … for practising English. You can find it at www.practiseagain.org

5 I've just watched a very funny … on YouTube.

8 My … battery has just stopped working, so I'm going to finish my homework on my computer at home.

9 Lim often … photos on our group chat.

3 **Read and complete the school rules for mobile phones. Use the words from the box.**

always   don't   keep   never   turn off

Mobile phone use in school

Please can all students read these rules about mobile phones in school.

You can bring your mobile phone to school, but …

- **1** _____ your phone when you get to school.

- **2** _____ it in your bag when you are in lessons.

- **3** _____ use your phone in lessons unless a teacher asks you to.

- **4** _____ send messages or call another student while they are in class.

- **5** _____ check you have your phone with you when you leave school.

4 **Write a blog post giving advice on mobile phones at home. Ideas you could include:**

- mealtimes
- family time e.g. watching films or playing games
- time spent on screens
- jobs you do at home
- homework
- going to sleep
- telling your parents where you are
- relaxing

_____
_____
_____
_____
_____
_____
_____
_____
_____
_____
_____

4.1 A healthy body

1 Say the words. Circle the silent letter in each one.

1 wrist

2 knee

3 stomach

2 Say the words. Which two words have the same vowel sound?

foot throat tooth toe

3 Read the article below about running. Complete the sentences with *mustn't / don't have to* or *should*.

1 You _____ wear good running shoes.

2 You _____ wear normal shoes.

3 You _____ go for a short run for five minutes the first time.

4 You _____ listen to music if you don't want to.

5 You _____ run after dinner.

6 You _____ take water with you when you run.

7 You _____ run too far the first time.

8 You _____ run with other people.

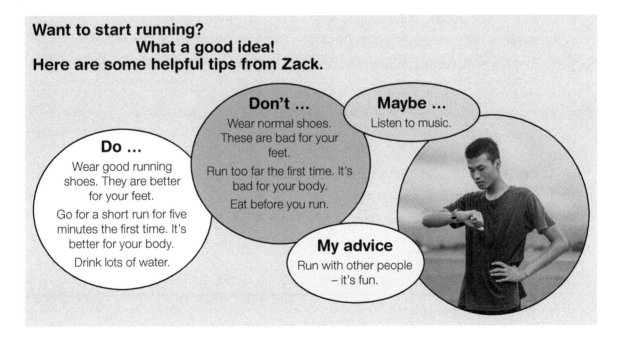

Want to start running?
What a good idea!
Here are some helpful tips from Zack.

Do ...
Wear good running shoes. They are better for your feet.
Go for a short run for five minutes the first time. It's better for your body.
Drink lots of water.

Don't ...
Wear normal shoes. These are bad for your feet.
Run too far the first time. It's bad for your body.
Eat before you run.

Maybe ...
Listen to music.

My advice
Run with other people – it's fun.

4 Put the letters in the correct order to make words.

1 gistnti	2 glapyin burgy	3 gojgign	4 inkringd twear
_____	_____	_____	_____

5 glapyin bablelskat	6 inkringd cefefo	7 ligcync
_____	_____	_____

5 Match the questions and answers. Practise saying these.

1 Can you run 10 kilometres in an hour?

2 Where can my daughter learn to play tennis?

3 How long can Tom and Ben cycle for?

4 What things can I do to get healthier?

5 Can Kai walk for longer than twenty minutes, doctor?

a They can ride for hours. They're really strong.

b A new club has just opened. She can play there.

c No, you can't. It's too far.

d Yes, he can try.

e You can swim or you can run or jog.

6 Complete the advice with the correct verbs in the box. Practise saying the advice.

drink sit start go try

1 Don't _____ too much coffee! It's not good for you.

2 _____ doing a new sport.

3 Don't _____ for too long at your desk!

4 _____ with five minutes and then do more the next day.

5 _____ to the gym and keep moving.

7 Your English cousin isn't very healthy. In your notebook, write an email to him / her giving advice how to be healthy.

4.2 Getting enough sleep

1 Write the words for the things in a bedroom.

1

_____

2

_____

3

_____

4

_____

5

_____

6

_____

2 Choose the correct options to complete Hui's online post.

I don't know what to do! I'm 15 years old. I have lots of friends and I chat online with them in the evenings. I **1** *go to bed / get up* at about 10.30 pm but I don't feel **2** *worse / tired*, so I often play some video games online or by myself. I usually **3** *feel / go* sleepy about two hours later, so I **4** *wake up / go to sleep* at about 12.30 am. I sleep very well until my alarm goes off at 6.45 am. I **5** *lie down / get up*, have a shower and eat breakfast and then I go to school. When I get to school at 8.45 I feel very **6** *sleepy / worse*. Some days I feel **7** *ill / better* and I have to go home at lunchtime. How can I sleep **8** *worse / better*?

3 Write a reply to Hui. Give him some advice.

_____
_____
_____
_____
_____

4 How can teenagers get enough sleep? Write a paragraph.

_____
_____
_____
_____
_____
_____

4.3 Getting better

1 **Match to make phrases.**

1	to do	**a**	your finger / your leg
2	to lie / fall	**b**	a headache / A toothache / a fever / a cold / an allergy
3	to cut	**c**	down
4	to be	**d**	thirsty / hungry / tired / ill
5	to have	**e**	exercise / sport

2 **Read the email. Decide if sentences 1–10 are true (T), false (F) or not mentioned (NM).**

Hi Juno,

How are you? I hope your weekend was good. My weekend wasn't great. I woke up on Saturday morning and I felt very tired, but I went to my swimming club. After swimming, I felt worse. I had a headache and a stomach ache. I went home and I lay down on my bed for an hour. I had a fever and my dad took me to the hospital. We had to wait for three hours to see the doctor. I was very thirsty and I drank four big bottles of water. The doctor was worried about me so I had to sleep at the hospital. On Sunday morning, I was feeling a bit better, so I came home. I can't go to school this week. I have to stay in bed. So please can you send me notes from the lessons?

Thanks,
Mia

1	Mia didn't go swimming at the weekend.	T / F / NM
2	She had a headache and a toothache.	T / F / NM
3	She had a fever.	T / F / NM
4	She didn't want to go to the hospital.	T / F / NM
5	At the hospital she was very hungry.	T / F / NM
6	The doctor was young.	T / F / NM
7	The doctor wasn't worried about Mia.	T / F / NM
8	Mia came home on Saturday.	T / F / NM
9	Mia has to do lots of exercise to feel better.	T / F / NM
10	She isn't going to school this week.	T / F / NM

3 **Correct the false sentences in activity 2.**

_____
_____
_____
_____
_____

4 **Look at this sentence from the text in activity 2. Practise saying it. Remember to make the underlined syllables sound stronger.**

I had a headache and a stomachache.

5 **Put the conversation in the correct order. Practise saying this.**

☐ **Mum:** Yes, of course. And you should go to bed.

1 **Yana:** Mum, I don't feel well.

☐ **Yana:** Yes, I am. Could you get me a drink, please?

☐ **Yana:** I feel hot and very tired.

☐ **Yana:** OK. Thanks, Mum.

☐ **Mum:** I think you have a fever. Are you thirsty?

☐ **Mum:** Oh no! What's wrong?

6 **Match the sentences 1–5 to the requests a–e. Practise saying these.**

1 These books are heavy.

2 I've got a headache.

3 I'm thirsty.

4 I'm late for school.

5 I'm cold.

a Could you drive me in the car, please?

b Could you speak more quietly, please?

c Could you get me a blanket, please?

d Could I have some water, please?

e Could you help me carry them, please?

7 **Complete the sentences with *could* or *please*. Practise saying these requests.**

1 _____ you stand up?

2 _____ could you open the window?

3 _____ you tell me what happened, _____?

4 Please _____ you show me the cut on your leg?

5 Could you carry these books, _____?

6 _____ _____ you wait here for a minute?

8 **For each sentence write R for request or A for advice. Practise saying these.**

1 You ought to go to the doctor's. _____

2 You shouldn't drink coffee in the evenings. _____

3 Could you open the door, please? _____

4 Could you tell me the time, please? _____

5 You ought to go to bed now. _____

6 You should do more exercise. _____

4.4 A healthy mind

1 Match the words to their definitions.

> active angry calm crying happy negative positive smiling

1 _____: not worried, angry or excited
2 _____: when you are confident and think things are good; the opposite of negative
3 _____: when tears are coming from your eyes because you are unhappy or hurt
4 _____: moving around a lot and doing lots of different things
5 _____: feeling pleased or satisfied
6 _____: feeling a strong negative emotion when someone has done something bad, or with something you don't like
7 _____: moving your mouth to show you are happy
8 _____: when you only see the bad side of a situation; the opposite of positive

2 Put the words from the box in activity 1 into the correct columns in the table.

One syllable	Two syllables	Three syllables

3 Complete the sentences with the verbs from the box in their correct form.

> breathe cry laugh smile think worry

1 In exams, I sometimes forget _____ and then my chest hurts.
2 I _____ about joining a football club. In your opinion, is it a good idea?
3 Don't _____ – you're not ill, you just need to relax more.
4 Yesterday when I got home from school my sister _____ because she was watching a sad film.
5 I _____ when my cat did a funny dance in the kitchen.
6 I don't like our new history teacher – he is very serious and never _____.

4 Answer the questions about you. Write complete sentences. Practise saying these.

1 What makes you laugh?

_____

2 What makes you cry?

_____

3 What do you worry about?

_____

4 When do you feel happy?

_____

5 Complete each sentence with an adverb of manner. Use the words in brackets.

1 The little girl was playing _____ by herself in the garden. **(happy)**

2 George plays cricket _____. **(good)**

3 The teacher _____ asked the class to be quiet. **(calm)**

4 Davood closed the door _____. **(angry)**

5 Yasmin looked up _____ from her textbooks. **(sleep)**

6 Kai plays the guitar _____. **(bad)**

7 Mimi walked away _____. **(sad)**

8 The man shouted _____ at the bus driver. **(crazy)**

9 Luke ran home _____. **(quick)**

10 Suzi tidied her bedroom _____. **(slow)**

6 Answer the questions about you. Write complete sentences. Practise saying these.

1 What do you do well?

_____

2 What do you do badly?

_____

3 What do you do quickly?

_____

4 What do you do slowly?

_____

7 Mum wants Mirra to help at home today. Write sentences about Mirra's jobs for today using *need to.*

1 ✓ **2** ✓ **3** ✓ **4** ✓

Today Mirra …

1 <u>needs to wash the car.</u> **2** _____

3 _____ **4** _____

4.5 Eating well

1 Choose the correct word for each photo.

1 milk / lemonade
2 peach / pear
3 raspberry / watermelon
4 cereal / salt
5 sugar / oil
6 cream / jelly

7 vegetables / fruit
8 lamb / burger
9 soft drink / coffee
10 yoghurt / jam
11 ice cream / jelly
12 strawberries / raspberries

2 Write the foods in activity 1 in the correct column in the table.

Countable	Uncountable	Countable or Uncountable

3 Read the texts. Answer the questions.

My favourite food is lamb with potatoes. I also like pizza. I don't really like vegetables or fruit, but sometimes I eat an apple or some watermelon. I love chocolate and I eat it everyday after football. I drink lots of water – two or three litres – when I play football. **Gustavo**

For breakfast I usually have fruit, yoghurt and nuts. Then I have egg or chicken salad for lunch and fish or chicken in the evening for dinner. I don't eat foods with sugar in them because I don't want to get fat. I don't drink much water but I do drink a lot of coffee. I don't like exercise so I can't eat too much unhealthy food. **David**

1 Who doesn't eat sugar? _____

2 Who does a lot of exercise? _____

3 Who eats the healthiest foods? _____

4 What do you think Gustavo ought to eat more of? _____

5 Who drinks the most coffee? _____

6 What do you think David could do to be healthier? _____

4 Write a paragraph about what you could do to be healthier.

_____

_____

_____

_____

_____

_____

5 Match the verbs with their past participles.

1	feed	**a**	closed
2	close	**b**	taken
3	put	**c**	encouraged
4	take	**d**	seen
5	tell	**e**	fed
6	encourage	**f**	lost
7	invite	**g**	drunk
8	lose	**h**	invited
9	see	**i**	put
10	drink	**j**	told
11	allow	**k**	driven
12	drive	**l**	allowed

6 Complete the sentences using the present passive of the verbs in brackets.

1 At our school, students _____ to do a lot of exercise. **(encourage)**

2 I _____ to a party on Friday night. **(invite)**

3 Students _____ to make an exam study timetable. **(tell)**

4 The cat _____ twice a day. **(feed)**

5 Exams _____ by students in Year 11. **(take)**

6 About 30 mobile phones _____ at school every year. **(lose)**

7 Many drinks cans _____ in the recycling bin. **(not put)**

8 The school gates _____ at 4 pm. **(close)**

9 Smoking _____ in school. **(not allow)**

10 Owls are birds which _____ at night. **(often see)**

11 Most of my friends _____ to school by their parents. **(drive)**

12 Different coffees _____ at different times of the day in Italy. **(drink)**

5.1 My neighbourhood

1 Write the words for places 1–10 on Hythe Road.

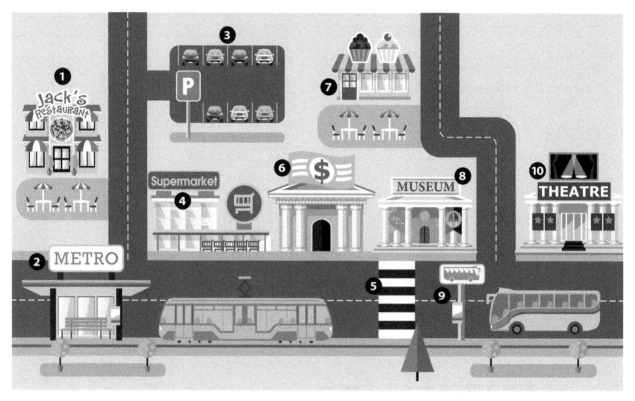

1 _____   2 _____   3 _____   4 _____

5 _____   6 _____   7 _____   8 _____

9 _____   10 _____

2 Decide if the sentences about Hythe Road in activity 1 are true (T) or false (F).

1 There are two places to eat on Hythe Road.   **T/F**

2 There isn't a cinema.   **T/F**

3 There isn't anywhere to leave your car.   **T/F**

4 There isn't anywhere to get money.   **T/F**

5 There aren't any traffic lights on Hythe Road.   **T/F**

6 There is a place to cross the road on Hythe Road.   **T/F**

3 Complete the sentences about Hythe Road with *is*, *isn't*, *are* or *aren't*.

1 There _____ a museum.

2 There _____ a bridge.

3 There _____ any tram stops.

4 There _____ any clothes shops.

5 There _____ a theatre.

4   **Match sentences 1–6 to places a–f.**

1   Jon wants to go to Newcastle.
2   Martha wants to buy some chicken for dinner.
3   Stefan wants to play tennis.
4   Lucca wants to talk to his history teacher.
5   Tomas wants to have a coffee and a sandwich.
6   Assia wants to see the animals.

a   the sports centre
b   the zoo
c   the cafe
d   the train station
e   the school
f   the butcher's

5   **Write the opposite words.**

1   a crowded street – an _e_ __ __ __ __ street
2   an old-fashioned building – a _m_ __ __ __ __ __ building
3   a narrow road – a _w_ __ __ __ road
4   a boring party – a _l_ __ __ __ __ __ party

6   **Choose the correct word for each photo.**

a   b   c   d   e

street / river   roundabout / bridge   pedestrian crossing / traffic lights   tram stop / bus stop   car park / metro station

7   **Complete the sentence with the words in the box.**

city   town   village

A ___town___ is smaller than a _____. But a _____ is smaller than a _____.

8   **Look at the photos and choose the correct options to complete the sentences.**

1   2   3   4   5

This / That is my notebook.   *These / Those* are my bags.   *These / Those* are lively monkeys.   *These / Those* are my friends.   *This / That* is a big bird.

9   **Answer the questions about you. Write complete sentences. Practise saying these.**

1   What did you use to think was boring that you don't think is boring now?

_____

2   What clothes did you use to wear that you don't wear now?

_____

3   What hobbies didn't you use to do that you do now?

_____

5.2 My favourite places

1 Write the words for the buildings. Then count the syllables in each word and write the number in the box.

1 _____ : a place where books, newspapers, DVDs and music are kept for people to use or borrow. ☐

2 _____ : a building where you can buy stamps and send letters. ☐

3 _____ : a place where aeroplanes come and go. ☐

4 _____ : a large building with thick, high walls that was built in the past to protect people. ☐

5 _____ : a place where people can keep their money. ☐

6 _____ : a place where you buy fuel for your car. ☐

7 _____ : a building where people pay to sleep and eat meals. ☐

8 _____ : a place that provides details of hotels and places to visit in an area to people who are visiting or on holiday. ☐

9 _____ : a large and important church. ☐

10 _____ : a place in a town or city where a lot of buses stop. ☐

11 _____ : a large sports pitch with lots of seats around it. ☐

12 _____ : a place where bread and cakes are baked or sold. ☐

13 _____ : a large building where people use machines to make things to sell. ☐

14 _____ : a place where doctors and nurses care for people who are ill or injured. ☐

15 _____ : a place where people get their cars fixed. ☐

16 _____ : a place where you go to have your hair cut. ☐

2 Look at the map of Hythe Road in 5.1 activity 1. Complete the dialogue with the words from the box. Practise saying the dialogue.

across   behind   next to   other   right

Guide: This is Hythe Road. It has some very interesting buildings. Do you have any questions?

Tourist 1: Yes! I need some money. Is there a bank?

Guide: Yes, the bank is **1** _____ the supermarket.

Tourist 2: And I'm hungry is there somewhere to eat?

Guide: Yes. There's a restaurant on the **2** _____ side of the supermarket. And there's a café **3** _____ the museum.

Tourist 3: Can I go to the cathedral?

Guide: Yes, the cathedral isn't on Hythe Road. You have to take a bus. There's a bus stop opposite the museum.

Tourist 4: Can I go to the castle?

Guide: Yes, of course. To get to the castle you should take the metro. The metro station is **4** _____ the road from the restaurant.

Tourist 5: And is there a theatre?

Guide: Yes, there is. It's the tall building on the **5** _____. Across the road from the museum.

3 Look at the map and choose the best words to complete the directions. Practise saying this.

Tourist: Excuse me, could you tell me how to get to the Shire Hotel, please?

Woman: Yes, of course. Leave the metro station and turn **1 left / right**. Walk to the roundabout and turn **2 left / right**. Go past the castle and **3 over / straight** the bridge. At the traffic lights, turn **4 left / right**. Walk past the stadium on your **5 left / right**. Turn right and then turn **6 left / right again**. Go **7 across / straight** on past the petrol station, the library on your left and the museum on your right, The Shire Hotel is at the **8 end / middle** of the road.

Tourist: Thank you.

4 Match the beginning of each sentence with the end of each sentence.

1 Jane's going to the garage
2 Mohammed's going to the café
3 My mum's at the hairdresser's
4 Kai went to the museum
5 Polly went to the bookshop

a to buy a book.
b having her hair cut.
c to have coffee with Sami.
d to see the paintings.
e to get her car repaired.

5 Write a reply to Emilia's text message. Tell her where you went in town today and why. Talk about three different places.

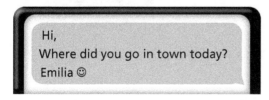

Hi,
Where did you go in town today?
Emilia ☺

5.3 Good neighbours

1 **Match the words to their meanings.**

> build gardening neighbour neighbourhood plant

1 _____: someone who lives near you

2 _____: to make something by joining different things together

3 _____: to put something into the ground so that it will grow

4 _____: doing work in a garden

5 _____: one of the parts of a town where people live

2 **Complete the sentences using the present continuous of the verbs in brackets.**

1 Judy _____ some flowers in her garden. **(plant)**

2 I _____ to the cinema. **(go)**

3 My grandparents _____ my uncle and aunt. **(visit)**

4 The class _____ a project about Australia. **(do)**

5 The teacher _____ us a video. **(show)**

6 We _____ a party. **(have)**

7 I _____ my bedroom. **(not tidy)**

8 My brothers and I _____ the bus to school. **(get)**

3 **Look at the pictures. Write the correct letter a–g to match sentences 1–5.**

Next week, Jem is helping in his neighbourhood.

1 He's planting a tree in the playground. ☐

2 He's showing some children how to plant vegetables. ☐

3 He's repairing a wall in the playground. ☐

4 He's helping at a picnic for the children and their families. ☐

5 And he's playing guitar and singing in a concert at the picnic. ☐

4 Write a sentence to say what Jem is also doing next week for the two other pictures in activity 2.

_____

_____

5 Read Ava's message and answer the questions.

Hi Joy

The school holidays start next week and I'm going to be very busy. My best friend and I are helping at our local children's centre. We're teaching the children to play football, tennis and volleyball. We're also painting a big painting on a wall with the children. We're planning to paint lots of different animals. We're also planting a new garden for the children and building a treehouse for them. What are you doing this summer?

Ava   ✓✓

1 When are the school holidays?

_____

2 Where is Ava working in the summer?

_____

3 Name **two** things Ava and her friend are doing at the children's centre.

_____

_____

6 Write a message to Ava. Tell her what you are planning to do in the summer holidays.

Hi Ava,

_____

_____

_____

_____

_____

_____

_____

_____

_____

_____

_____

_____

_____

_____

5.4 My region

1 Say the words in the box and write them in the correct columns in the table.

desert forest island mountain river volcano waterfall

Oo	oOo	Ooo

2 Answer the questions about the words in activity 1.

1 Which two words have silent letters? What are the letters? _____ _____
2 Which word, wood or coast, has a long 'o' sound? _____
3 Which two words have the same long 'a' sound from waterfall, lake and volcano?
_____ _____

3 Put the words in the correct order to make sentences.

1 holiday / I'm / to / on / going / Greece

_____

2 hiking / probably / go / I / will

_____

3 staying / in / hotel / coast / on / I / the / am / a

_____

4 send / you / I / postcard / will / a

_____

5 home / I / on / 22nd / will / be / the

_____

6 we / cinema / shall / on / go / the / to / 23rd / the / ?

_____

4 Complete the conversations using *will*, *shall* or the present continuous of the verbs in brackets. Practise saying these.

A

Girl: Mum, would you be able to drive me to Luisa's house on Saturday evening at 8.00, please? Luisa **1** _____ **(have)** a birthday party.

Mum: I'm sorry, but your dad and I **2** _____ **(go)** to a restaurant for dinner at 7.00 in the city so we **3** _____ **(probably leave)** at 6.00.

B

Joe: What **4** _____ **(you do)** this weekend, Auntie Pauline?

Auntie Pauline: I don't know. Perhaps we **5** _____ **(go)** to the theatre.

Joe: Wow! Lucky you!

Auntie Pauline: **6** _____ **(I buy)** a ticket for you, too?

Joe: Yes, please!

C

Fiona: Hi, Dad – you look tired.

Dad: I am!

Fiona: **7** _____ **(I make)** you a cup of tea?

Dad: Yes, please.

Fiona: And I **8** _____ **(cook)** dinner for you, too!

Dad: Thanks, Fiona.

B

Maryam: **9** _____ **(you get)** the bus home after school, Hoda?

Hoda: Yes, I am. Are you?

Maryam: Yes, **10** _____ **(we meet)** at the canteen and get the bus together?

Hoda: Good idea! I **11** _____ **(be)** there at 4.15.

---

5 Answer the questions about you. Write complete sentences. Practise saying these.

1 What won't you do after school on Monday?

_____

2 What subjects do you think you will do at college?

_____

3 What do you think you will do in the summer holidays?

_____

5.5 I care about the environment

1 Choose the correct word for each photo.

1

land / cloud

2

sun / sea

3

recycling / wind farm

4

pollution / farming

5

sky / land

6
recycling / climate change

2 Underline the phrasal verbs in these sentences.

1 Let's find out some information for our project in the library.

2 Steffi can't come to football today because she's looking after her younger brother.

3 I always have a cup of coffee when I wake up.

4 My baby cousin is growing up very quickly.

3 Write the words in the correct order to make sentences.

1 the / the / teacher / to / class / listened

_____

2 my / I / talked / grandmother / to / the phone / for / an hour / on

_____

3 they care / don't / environment / the / about

_____

4 my / at / smiles / baby / everyone / sister

_____

5 Jordan / for / the / asked / menu

_____

4 Complete the sentences with the correct dependent prepositions.

> about (×2) at in of

1 Taylor is very excited _____ his school trip to the coast.

2 Harry is really good _____ geography.

3 Are you interested _____ travel?

4 Simi is frightened _____ spiders.

5 I'm worried _____ my exams next week.

5 Answer the questions. Write complete sentences. Practise saying these.

1 What are you worried about?

_____

2 What are you frightened of?

_____

3 What are you good at?

_____

4 What are you excited about?

_____

5 What did you learn about at school last week?

_____

6 Read Sol's email to her teacher. Complete the reported speech sentences.

Dear Miss Grange,

I am really sorry but I can't come on the school trip to the Wind Farm. I don't feel well. I am really sad because I really want to go. I'm staying in bed today.

I have a really bad headache!! I can't sit on a school bus for an hour.

Thank you.

Sol

1 Sol said that she _____ come on the school trip.

2 She said that she _____ feel well.

3 She said that she _____ really sad because she really _____ to go.

4 She said that she _____ _____ in bed today.

5 She said that she _____ a really bad headache.

6 She said that she _____ sit on a school bus for an hour.

6.1 The natural world

1 Answer the questions. Write complete sentences. Practise saying these.

1 Where do you live?

_____

2 What country were you born in?

_____

3 What is your nationality?

_____

4 What languages do you speak?

_____

5 What countries have you been to?

_____

2 Circle the correct words.

1 duck / snake   2 lion / tiger   3 dinosaur / elephant   4 sheep / cow   5 monkey / fly   6 bear / chicken

3 Complete the sentences using the superlative form of the adjectives in brackets.

1 The Nile is _____ river in the world. **(long)**

2 Athens is the capital of Greece and it is one of _____ cities in the world. **(old)**

3 The blue whale is _____ animal in the world. It weighs 180 tons. **(heavy)**

4 Russia is _____ country in the world. **(large)**

5 I think English is _____ language to learn. **(difficult)**

6 I think _____ beaches in the world are in South-East Asia. **(beautiful)**

4 Choose the correct word to complete each sentence.

1 Janis thought that she _might / perhaps_ be late for dinner.

2 When Iris saw the baby tiger she thought that the mother tiger was _could / probably_ near.

3 You've got a text message – it _possibly / may_ be from your mum.

4 This bone _could / perhaps_ be from a dinosaur.

5 The baby is crying – she's _might / probably_ hungry.

6 'Where are the lions?' ' I don't know. _Perhaps / Might_ they're sleeping.'

7 Today is _possibly / might be_ the hottest day of the year.

8 Don't worry, you will _possibly / definitely_ pass the exam.

6.2 What's the weather like?

1 **Complete the crossword.**

Across →

2 the opposite of hot
4 the very bright lights in the sky that happen in a storm
7 water that falls from the clouds
8 water that is frozen
9 very bad weather, with lots of rain and bad winds
10 soft white frozen water that falls from the sky
11 wet and warm weather

Down ↓

1 thick cloud that is close to the ground
3 a unit for measuring temperature
5 the loud noise you sometimes hear from the sky in a storm
6 air that moves
9 the light and heat that comes from the sun

2 **Write a paragraph describing the weather today.**

_____
_____
_____
_____

3 Match the sentence halves.

1 If it rains tomorrow,
2 If it's sunny at the weekend,
3 If the restaurant is closed,
4 If you can't do your homework,
5 I'll take a jumper and a coat
6 The neighbours will water our plants
7 If we go to Australia,
8 We'll go to Disneyland

a we'll go to the beach.
b I'll help you.
c if it's cold tomorrow.
d if we go to America.
e we won't go hiking.
f I'll cook dinner at my house.
g if we go on holiday.
h we'll visit Aunty Grace in Sydney.

4 Join the sentences using the first conditional.

1 You don't go on the bus. Your mum will have to drive you to school.
   If you don't go on the bus, your mum will have to drive you to school.

2 Mary goes to Egypt. She will see the pyramids.
   _____

3 You will get wet. It rains.
   _____

4 You see the new baby. Will you take a photo?
   _____

5 They won't call. They get home late.
   _____

6 You see Dan. Give him his phone, please?
   _____

5 Complete these sentences using the first conditional.

1 If you don't go to school, _____
2 If I go to New York in America, _____
3 If my family moves to another country, _____
4 If a new student starts at my school, _____
5 I'll go to university _____
6 I'll buy my friend a present _____

6 Choose the best phrase to complete the sentences.

   too expensive   too heavy   too loud   too small   too strong

1 I can't carry this suitcase it is _____.
2 The music was _____ so we left the party.
3 The wind was _____ so we couldn't go out.
4 The restaurant was _____ and we didn't have enough money.
5 She didn't buy the trainers because they were _____.

6.3 Where would you like to go?

1 Complete the sentences with the words from the box.

although and because but or so unless

1 I can't go to the party _____ I have lots of homework to do.

2 I can't go to the party _____ I finish my homework.

3 I'd like to go to India _____ I'd like to go to Africa.

4 I'd like to go to Europe _____ I wouldn't like to go to North America.

5 Shall we go skiing _____ sailing?

6 Let's go to the coast _____ we can go sailing.

7 Marco loves the sea _____ he can't swim.

2 Complete the conversations using *Shall* and *Let's*. Practise saying these.

A

Mum: Hey, Jen. **1** _____ we look for a dress online tonight for your end of school party?

Jen: Yes, please!

Mum: Which website do you want to look at?

Jen: Ummm... **2** _____ look at the Tara website.

B

Olivia: **3** _____ have dinner in a restaurant tonight.

Hugo: Good idea! **4** _____ go to that new restaurant in town.

Olivia: Yes, it looks like a nice place. **5** _____ I ring up and book a table?

---

3 Order the conversation. Practise saying this.

☐ **Julio:** Well, shall we do something inside, then?

1 **Pan:** What shall we do this weekend, Julio?

☐ **Julio:** I don't know! Let's do something fun. Let's play golf.

☐ **Pan:** Yes, let's go to the cinema.

☐ **Pan:** That's a great idea! Shall we both choose our favourite old film?

☐ **Julio:** Yes, and shall I bring some drinks?

☐ **Pan:** We could... but the weather's not very good.

☐ **Julio:** No, I've seen all the new films. I know – let's go to my house and watch an old film we both like.

☐ **Pan:** Yes, please. Shall I bring some snacks? I can bring chocolate and crisps.

4 Say the words in the box and write them in the correct columns in the table.

television cooker fridge iron telephone freezer
barbecue dishwasher oven microwave

One syllable	Two syllables	Three syllables	Four syllables

5 Look at the pictures. Write the correct letter a–f to match sentences 1–5. There is one picture you do not need.

a

b

c

d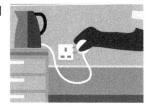

e

f

Raj is staying in a hotel.

1 His room has a fridge.　☐

2 It has electricity.　☐

3 It has an iron.　☐

4 It has wi-fi.　☐

5 But it doesn't have any heating.　☐

6.4 A school trip

1 Look at the photos and put the letters in the correct order to make words.

1
pac _____

2
lumberla _____

3
kicett _____

4
abckcapk _____

5
trainoca _____

6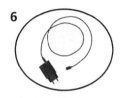
oneph gracher _____

7
tha _____

8
glup _____

9
prosts tik _____

10
sortpasp _____

11
miwsmngi sometuc
_____

12
ite _____

13
dricet drac _____

14
slogve _____

15
lochos muofirn
_____

16
debokguoi _____

2 Read the notice. Answer the questions about the school trip.

Year 11 school culture trip

This year the school culture trip is a six-day trip to Sri Lanka in Asia. We are going to visit a museum, a fishing town and a secondary school. And we will watch a dance performance by the students.

If you are interested, come to the meeting in the sports hall on Monday lunchtime.

1 What sort of school trip is it?

_____

2 How long is the school trip for?

_____

3 Which country are they going to?

_____

4 Which continent are they going to?

_____

5 What three places are they visiting?

_____

6 What are they going to watch?

_____

7 Where is the meeting about the trip?

_____

3 Match the sentence halves.

1 What's the name of the teacher
2 Is this the shop
3 These are the shoes
4 Are you the person
5 I have a friend

a where you bought your new necklace?
b who asked for a coffee with milk?
c that the queen wore at her wedding.
d who takes part in tennis competitions.
e who taught you English last year?

4 Complete the headteacher, Mr Perks', presentation notes about the school trip in activity 2. Use the relative pronouns *who*, *where* and *that*. Then answer the questions.

Good afternoon Year 11s. It's great to see so many of you are interested in the school trip to Sri Lanka. I have some photos to show you of the places we are going to go on the trip.

Slide 1: OK, so this is Colombo, a big city **1** _____ is also the capital of Sri Lanka. The hotel **2** _____ we are going to stay is very nice and you will share a room with one other student. We have booked a special coach to take us around the country. We will have our own driver **3** _____ will drive us to all the places we are going to visit on our trip. His name is Anvit and he speaks English.

Slide 2: So, we'll have a day to relax at the hotel and then we'll go to the national museum **4** _____ we will learn about the history of Sri Lanka. It's a very interesting museum and students usually enjoy the visit.

Slide 3: The next day we'll go to the town of Galle **5** _____ fishermen use traditional boats to catch fish. Here you can see the traditional fishing boats **6** _____ are used in Sri Lanka. You can try the fresh fish at the local restaurant we'll go to.

Slide 4: Finally, there is a very good secondary school **7** _____ we will visit for the last two days. You will go to some lessons and talk to the students about their lives and yours. These are some of the students **8** _____ you will meet. And some children from the school will perform a dance show for us on our last night in Sri Lanka. I hope you will make friends with them.

9 What is the name of the coach driver?

_____

10 Where will they go to eat fish?

_____

11 How many days will they visit the school for?

_____

6.5 Let's go!

1 Match sentences 1–8 to photo A or B.

A

B

1	The passenger is at the airport.	A	B
2	The passenger has a backpack.	A	B
3	There's a platform.	A	B
4	The passenger is at the railway station.	A	B
5	There's a plane.	A	B
6	The passenger has a suitcase.	A	B
7	The passenger is going on a flight.	A	B
8	There's a train.	A	B

2 Complete the sentences using the verbs from the box. Use the correct forms.

arrive   be lost   cross   be delayed   depart   drive   fly   look forward to   miss   park   rent

1 Does the train to Bangkok _____ at 1 pm and _____ at Chang Mai at 5 pm?

2 'Where are you, Dad?' 'I'm here – I _____ the car.'

3 'Is Dave _____ the holiday?'

4 Polly arrived half an hour late at the airport so she _____ her flight.

5 'Sorry, Stefan, I can't find the railway station. I don't know where I am – I think I _____.'

6 We never _____ to my grandparents' house because it's too far and our car is quite old.

7 My best friend won't _____ because she hates planes.

8 We want to drive around the country, so we _____ a car at the airport.

9 Come out of the exit and _____ the road.

10 When we flew back from Miami last month, the plane _____ for four hours!

3 Read the details of a new art course. Write the questions.

ART WORKSHOP

New Art Class – everyone is welcome

Come and join us every Wednesday from 4.30 pm to 6.30 pm for two hours of art from the 1st of July to the 1st of September at the Guildhall.

1 <u>What date does the class start?</u>

On the 1st of July.

2 _____

On the 1st of September.

3 _____

Wednesdays.

4 _____

At 4.30 pm.

5 _____

At 6.30 pm.

4 Answer the questions for you. Use the present simple to talk about the future. Practise saying these.

1 What month is it next month?

_____

2 What is the date next Friday?

_____

3 When are your next exams?

_____

4 What time does school start tomorrow?

_____

5 When do the school holidays start?

_____

6 When is your birthday?

_____

7 How old are you on your next birthday?

_____

7.1 I'm good at English

1 Choose the correct words A, B or C to complete Farah's email.

Hi Granddad

How are you? I hope you're well.

I'm writing to tell you about my new school. It's a big school, but it's nice. The other
1 _____ are friendly and I'm sure I'll make some good friends soon. We have six
2 _____ a day: three before lunch and three more in the afternoon. My favourite
3 _____ is maths, and I also like chemistry and physics. My maths **4** _____
is called Mr Pinter. He's very kind and funny, so his **5** _____ are fun. But he does
give us a lot of **6** _____ – I have two hours to do this evening!

See you soon ☺
Farah

1 A director	**B** students	**C** teachers
2 A lessons	**B** classrooms	**C** homework
3 A subject	**B** teacher	**C** school
4 A class	**B** homework	**C** teacher
5 A students	**B** classes	**C** classrooms
6 A homework	**B** subjects	**C** time

2 Write the school each person goes to.

1 Victor is fourteen years old. He goes to _____.

2 Liz is twenty years old. She is studying at _____.

3 Nathan is eight years old. He is at _____.

4 Layla is three and a half years old. She goes to _____.

3 Complete the adjectives.

1 We had an i _ _ _ _ _ _ t _ _ _ biology lesson today – I learnt a lot.

2 Can you please help me with my homework? It's very d _ _ _ _ _ _ _ t.

3 I'm very b _ _ at geography.

4 I'm not interested in drama – I think it's bor _ _ _.

4 Complete each sentence with the correct form of the verbs in brackets.

1 OK class, can anyone _____ question 5? **(answer)**

2 If you don't _____ notes, you won't remember what I say. **(take)**

3 Susan _____ the biology test. **(fail)**

4 Mohammed _____ an interesting essay about world religions. **(write)**

5 Did Jeremy _____ his driving test? **(pass)**

5 **Put the words in the correct order to make sentences.**

1 play / guitar / can / Herbie / the

_____

2 Kimmy / horse / a / ride / can't

_____

3 I / bike / couldn't / when / five / was / a / ride / I

_____

4 Joan / couldn't / teacher / the / hear

_____

5 can't / phone / her / find / Grandma

_____

6 you / speak / Can / German / ?

_____

6 **Complete the sentences using *can, can't, could* or *couldn't*.**

1 Mr Osman wears glasses because he _____ see very well.

2 'The maths homework is very difficult.' 'Judy _____ help you – she's very good at maths.'

3 Yesterday, Rufus _____ go to the gym because he was sick.

4 Mina is very clever – she _____ read before she was four.

5 I'm 15 so I _____ drive yet.

6 I _____ swim until I was ten.

7 **Complete each sentence with an adverb of manner. Use the adjectives in the brackets. Then match the photos with the sentences.**

a   b   c

d   e   f

1 Cooper walked _____ to his car. **(slow)**

2 The teacher spoke very _____ to Maryam. **(quiet)**

3 Monty ran _____ across the park when he saw me. **(quick)**

4 Our football team played very _____ today. They won the match. **(good)**

5 The children were playing _____ outside all afternoon. **(happy)**

6 The snake moved _____ through the grass. **(silent)**

7.2 How to be a good student

1 Underline the best verb to complete each sentence. Practise saying these.

1 I like to *study / explain / understand* in the school library.
2 I hope I *try / get / know* a good mark for my English essay.
3 Do you want to *revise / explain / try* for our maths exam at my house?
4 Do you *explain / practise / know* how to do this experiment?
5 Please can you *explain / study / revise* the homework again Miss Clare?

2 Look at the pictures. Write the correct letter a–f to match sentences 1–5.

a

b

c

d

e

f

Una …

1 has cooked dinner. ☐
2 has painted a picture of a flower. ☐
3 has made a cake. ☐
4 has written a letter to her grandparents. ☐
5 has fed the rabbit. ☐

3 Complete the sentence for the extra picture in activity 2.

Una _____

_____

4 Make sentences about Nora, Viktor and Izzy. Use the information in the table. Use the present perfect.

	travel to Africa	ride an elephant	stay up all night to watch the sunrise	eat Caribbean food	drive a motorbike
Nora	✗	✗	✓	✗	✓
Viktor	✓	✓	✓	✗	✗
Izzy	✓	✗	✓	✓	✗

Example: Nora hasn't travelled to Africa. Viktor and Izzy have travelled to Africa.

1 _____

2 _____

3 _____

4 _____

5 Write sentences about yourself using the activities in the table in activity 4. Practise saying these.

_____

_____

_____

_____

6 Complete the sentences with *ever* or *never*.

1 I've _____ seen a bear.

2 Have you _____ been to Disneyland?

3 Has Mrs Baker _____ taught geography?

4 Kai's _____ come to my house.

5 Have your parents _____ left you home alone?

7 Complete the conversations.

A: Hi Luke, have you seen Mrs Knight?

B: No, I **1** _____.

C: Chiara, have you read this book?

D: Yes, I **2** _____.

E: Has Elliot phoned you?

F: No, he **3** _____.

G: Has Dina finished her homework?

H: Yes, she **4** _____.

7.3 A great school

1 Complete the crossword.

Clues

Across

2 a space outside a school building where students can spend their breaks

4 the most important teacher in the school

6 the marks you get at the end of a test or an exam

Down

1 a place in a school or a university where students can buy and eat lunch

3 the special clothes that some students wear to school

5 all the things that are used for a particular purpose

2 Choose the correct adjective to complete each sentence.

1 Javid was *satisfied / satisfying* with the mark he got for his project.

2 The online art course is very *interested / interesting*.

3 I'm *surprised / surprising* that I got 100% in the test.

4 PE was *tired / tiring* today.

5 If I study for more than one hour, I get *bored / boring*.

6 Revision is *exhausted / exhausting*!

3 Read the text and answer the questions.

I go to an English-speaking private secondary school. It's a lovely school. One part of the school is very old and it has a lot of small classrooms. It has a library and some nice drama and music rooms. The other part was built in 2020. The new building has a lot of bigger rooms and there is also an amazing new gym. I've had some classes in the new building, but not many. We go there to eat because that's where the canteen is, too. It's very big with lots of tables and chairs, so we meet all our friends there at lunchtime. Classes are quite small. We usually have 15 students in each class although the religious studies classes are larger with about 25 students in each class. There are quite a lot of school trips. I've been on four school trips already this term. They're very tiring and I don't think they are very interesting or useful.

1 What language is spoken at the school?

_____

2 How many school buildings does the school have?

_____

3 When was the new building built?

_____

4 Where is the library?

_____

5 Where is the gym?

_____

6 Where is the canteen?

_____

7 How many students are there in most classes?

_____

8 Which subject has more students in each class?

_____

9 What does the writer think about school trips?

_____

4 Write a paragraph about a school trip you have been on. Where did you go? What did you do? How was it? How did you feel on the trip?

_____

_____

_____

_____

_____

7.4 Different types of schools

1 Put the words in the correct order to make sentences.

1 the / for / I / French / had / same / teacher / years / have / three

_____

2 aunt / since / summer / We / my / the / haven't / seen

_____

3 long / have / for / How / here / lived / you / ?

_____

4 Yuri / violin / since / was / has / four / played / the / he

_____

5 7 o'clock / been / The / asleep / since / children / have

_____

6 waited / Jenny / two hours / for / I / for / went / home / then / I

_____

2 Complete the sentences using the present perfect and *for* or *since*. Use the verbs in brackets.

1 Britta _____ her horse _____ two and a half years. **(have)**

2 June _____ the colour of her hair _____ I last saw her. **(change)**

3 My cousin Ferdie and I _____ _____ he was rude to me at his brother's wedding. **(not speak)**

4 I _____ to the cinema _____ a month. **(not go)**

5 My father _____ _____ two days. **(not sleep)**

6 My grandad _____ by himself _____ 2010. **(live)**

3 Write answers that are true for you. Practise saying these.

1 How long have you lived in your house?

_____

2 How long have you been at your school?

_____

3 How long have you studied English?

_____

4 How long have you known your best friend?

_____

4 **Match the conjunctions to their meanings.**

as soon as   after   before   until   when   while

1 _____: earlier than
2 _____: not after this time
3 _____: later than
4 _____: at the same time
5 _____: immediately after

5 **Look at the pictures and make sentences using the words in brackets.**

1 (I / Tim / present / as soon as / arrive / party)

_____

_____

2 (I / TV / while / eat dinner)

_____

_____

3 (Nasser / teeth / before / go / bed)

_____

_____

4 (Mum / be / in a bad mood / until / Dad / make her laugh)

_____

_____

7.5 Online lessons

1   **Choose the best word for each picture.**

a keyboard / printer / folder

b speaker / touchscreen / memory stick

c tablet / speaker / printer

d laptop / keyboard / printer

e email / memory stick / tablet

f keyboard / memory stick / screen

g mail / tablet / upload

h tablet / folder / memory stick

i folders / speakers / laptops

j screen / folder / email

k download / email / upload

l speaker / printer / laptop

m mail / folder / document

2 Cross out the word in each sentence that is in the wrong place.

1 Baz has just left ~~just~~.

2 Grace ~~yet~~ hasn't seen my new speakers yet.

3 Lacey still hasn't returned ~~still~~ her library book.

4 I've already eaten ~~already~~ my lunch.

5 They ~~just~~ have just called.

6 Joe still hasn't uploaded the photos ~~still~~.

3 Write sentences about the things Jay has and hasn't done before school. Use the present perfect and *yet* or *already*.

find pencil case	✗
make lunch	✓
put shoes on	✗
clear the breakfast table	✗
brush hair	✗
text friend	✓

1 Jay hasn't found his pencil case yet.

2 _____

3 _____

4 _____

5 _____

6 _____

4 Write sentences about the things Lenora has and hasn't done after school. Use the present perfect and *just* or *still*.

do chemistry homework	✗
have coffee with a friend	✓
have a shower	✗
watch a film	✓
call Granny	✗
give the rabbit its food	✗

1 Lenora still hasn't done her chemistry homework.

2 _____

3 _____

4 _____

5 _____

6 _____

8.1 Jobs

1 Choose the correct option for each conversation.

1

> *Are you going to go / Do you go* to the football match tonight?

> Yes, I am. I have two tickets but Sally can't go. Do you want one?

2

> *I'm cooking / I will cook* lunch on Sunday at 2 o'clock. Can you come?

> Thanks, but I'm meeting my cousin in the afternoon.

3

> How old *are you / will you be* in December?

> *I'll be / I am* sixteen. How about you?

4

> What time *is the concert going to finish / does the concert finish*?

> It *is finishing / finishes* at about 11.30.

2 Write the answers to the questions using the words in brackets.

1 What are you doing tomorrow?

_____ (I / go / school)

2 What time does school finish tomorrow?

_____ (It / finish / 3pm)

3 When do your summer holidays end?

_____ (they / finish / September 3rd)

4 Are you going to go to university / college when you finish school?

_____ (Yes / go / to / New York University)

5 What are you going to study?

_____ (I / study / French)

6 Are you going get a job in the summer?

_____ (No / get / job / summer)

7 How old will you be on 1st February next year?

_____ (I / be / seventeen)

8 What won't you do next week? Why not?

_____ (I / not / study / because / I / be / on vacation)

3 Write the questions for these answers.

1 _____ ?

I'll be 21 next April.

2 _____ ?

Yes, I am going to the concert tonight.

3 _____ ?

I start my job at 9 am in the morning.

4 _____ ?

No, I'm not going to get a new job next year.

5 _____ ?

My holidays start in April this year.

6 _____ ?

No, I'm not doing anything tonight.

7 _____ ?

I'll arrive at the airport at 6:30 am.

8 _____ ?

Yes, she is going to look for a job this summer.

4 Look at the pictures and match them with the descriptions. Write the names of the jobs next to the descriptions.

a   b   c   d   e

f   g   h   i   j

1 You do this job inside and you clean things.	*e* — *cleaner*
2 This is a dangerous job and you have to put out fires.	☐ _____
3 I think this is quite an exciting job. You often act in films.	☐ _____
4 You work outside and often work with animals.	☐ _____
5 You do this job in a plane. You look after people and give them food and drinks.	☐ _____
6 You work long hours in this job and you drive a big type of vehicle.	☐ _____
7 You work in a hospital and help sick people.	☐ _____
8 In this job you use a camera to take pictures.	☐ _____
9 You make bread for customers.	☐ _____
10 You build houses and other things.	☐ _____

5 Put the words in the correct order to make the sentences. Finish them. Then practise saying these.

1 would / I / to / love / actor / an / be _____

2 really / would / I / a / to / like / be / nurse _____

3 I / with / would / to / like / work / children? _____

4 like / I / wouldn't / attendant / a / be / to / flight _____

5 really / mechanic / I / be / wouldn't / to / a / like _____

6 a / to / I / would / be / cleaner / hate _____

6 Match the sentence halves.

1 Joe would really like to be a lawyer ...

2 Zach would really hate to be a nurse ...

3 Stella would really like to be a teacher ...

4 Greta would like to be a flight attendant ...

5 Henri would like to be a vet because ...

6 Sara wouldn't like to be a singer because ...

a ... because she wants to travel.

b ... because he loves animals.

c ... because it is well-paid.

d ... because she loves children.

e ... because he doesn't like hospitals.

f ... because she doesn't want to be famous.

7 Write a sentence for each job. Why would you like to do this job? Why wouldn't you like to do this job? Practise saying these.

Use: *would / wouldn't / like / hate / because*

artist   baker   bus driver   cleaner   manager   photographer

1 _____

2 _____

3 _____

4 _____

8.2 The world of work

1 Read the text and choose the best options.

> I would like **1** _____ a boss, and I would like the
> opportunity **2** _____ in a big company in the USA.
> I have a lot of skills. For example, I'm good **3** _____
> languages and I'm good at working **4** _____ other
> people. Also, I am **5** _____ and hard-working. My dad has
> a business and I have **6** _____ helped him in the office
> in the summer holidays, so I know about working hard and
> working with other people. I would like to be **7** _____
> businesswoman in the world but I will need more **8** _____.

1	**A** be	**B** to be	**C** to being
2	**A** working	**B** work	**C** to work
3	**A** with	**B** in	**C** at
4	**A** with	**B** to	**C** of
5	**A** friends	**B** friendly	**C** friend
6	**A** often	**B** never	**C** ever
7	**A** best	**B** better	**C** the best
8	**A** hours	**B** experience	**C** rich

2 Complete the sentences with the correct phrasal verb.

> find out   look after   pick up   put on   turn on   put out

1 I often _____ _____ people in my taxi from the airport.

2 You need to _____ _____ some sun cream. It's very hot today.

3 Can you please _____ _____ the children? I have to go out for five minutes.

4 I want to _____ _____ about how to get a part-time job.

5 Please _____ _____ that fire. You mustn't light any fires on the beach.

6 Be careful when you _____ _____ the tap. The water is very hot.

3 Complete the sentences with the infinitive of purpose of the verbs in the box.

> buy   earn   find   meet   learn   work

1 Jemma went to evening classes _____ Chinese.

2 I'm looking for a job at the weekends _____ some extra money while I study.

3 Fernando is going to America in July _____ at a summer camp.

4 My sister is saving _____ a house.

5 Billy is going to join a sports club _____ some new people.

6 I did an online course in computing _____ a better job.

8.3 Applying for jobs

 1 Read the text and decide if the sentences are true (T) or false(F).

17a Calle Unidad
Madrid
Spain

anaruiz123@mediamail.com

Dear Mrs Sanchez

I am writing to apply for the job of Spanish teacher at the London School of Languages.

My name is Ana Ruiz. I am a young Spanish woman living in the capital of Spain, Madrid. I was born on 29th October 1997 and I speak fluent English, French and Spanish. I have a degree in languages from the University of Seville and I have been a primary school teacher for 2 years. I love working with young children because they are so interested in the world and love learning new things.

I am looking for a new job in England. I would love to have the opportunity to work in London because I would like to get more experience teaching in an international school.

I am friendly, polite and I work well in a team. I also have a driver's licence, a first-aid certificate and good computer skills. My CV is attached to this letter.

I look forward to hearing from you.

Yours sincerely

Ana Ruiz

1 Ana is English.   T/F
2 She lives in Spain.   T/F
3 Her birthday is in October.   T/F
4 She can speak two languages.   T/F
5 She doesn't like working with young children.   T/F
6 She wants to work in another country.   T/F
7 She can drive a car.   T/F
8 She would like to learn how to become a teacher.   T/F

2 Read the text again and complete Ana's CV.

Name: Miss _____

Date of Birth: _____

Nationality: _____

Address: _____

Email: _____

Skills: _____ driver's licence, a _____ certificate and good
computer skills

Qualifications: _____

Experience: _____ as primary school teacher

3 Complete the advice for getting a job. Use the words from the box.

Firstly   Finally   Next   Secondly

Here are some things you can do to help you get job. **1** _____, you should look at job
advertisements and find a job you think you can do. **2** _____ you need to write a CV
with your personal details, experience and skills. For example, if it is a job in a café, you
might say that you have helped your mum make drinks at family parties. **3** _____ read
your CV carefully to make sure you haven't made any spelling mistakes. **4** _____, send
your CV with a letter or email to the employer and wait for a reply. Good luck!

4 Choose the best option.

1 You **should** / **could** tell your boss you really need a holiday.

2 If you want to earn more money, you **ought to** / **can** look for a new job.

3 She **ought to** / **could** take the train or the bus, they both take the same amount of time.

4 I know I **should** / **could** stop eating junk food.

5 Do you know where I **can** / **should** find a part-time job?

6 On your CV you **need to** / **could** include your personal details.

5 Match the vowel sounds in words 1–2 to the same sounds a–b.

1 **ou**ght   a d**oo**r

2 c**ou**ld   b g**oo**d

6 Circle the silent letter in these words.

could   should

8.4 Starting a business

1 Choose the correct options: A, B or C for each sentence. Practise saying these.

1 Excuse me! There isn't a _____ on these glasses. How much are they?

2 I'd like a _____. This coffee tastes terrible!

3 Hello. How much is it to _____ a car for the day?

4 That's £12.50 please. Would you like a _____?

5 I'd like to pay this money into my bank _____, please.

6 Excuse me? Could you give some _____ for this 50 euros?

1	**A** price	**B** receipt	**C** rent
2	**A** change	**B** refund	**C** receipt
3	**A** rent	**B** change	**C** refund
4	**A** price	**B** account	**C** receipt
5	**A** refund	**B** rent	**C** account
6	**A** change	**B** refund	**C** receipt

2 Complete the text with the words from the box. There is one word you do not need.

holidays   money   retire   salary   unemployed

My name is Jack, and I live in Rome, the capital of Italy. Last year I was **1** _____ for six months because my job ended. So, I looked for a new job. I wanted a job with a good **2** _____, so I decided to study English to help me find a better job. Now I am a guide. I look after tourists and show them my beautiful city. It is the best job I have ever had. I also get paid **3** _____, which is great. This means I can relax and go to the beach. I hope I can work as a guide for many years. In the future I'd like to **4** _____ and grow vegetables in my garden and watch my grandchildren grow up.

3 Write a reported command for each sentence.

1 "Answer the phone," Ben said to me.

He _____.

2 "Don't reply to the email," she said to me.

She _____.

3 "Wait for me at the station at 8 o'clock," Dad told us.

Dad _____.

4 "Take a holiday," my boss said to Jane.

My _____.

8.5 Thinking about the future

1 Read the conversation and choose the correct option. Practise saying this conversation.

Sam: We've finished school!

Carlos: Yes! I can't believe it!

Sam: What **1 *do we* / *are we going*** to do all summer?

Carlos: I want to do nothing at all!

Sam: **2 *Aren't you going to* / *Wouldn't you*** get a job?

Carlos: No! My mum is going to give me some money.

Sam: Lucky you! I need a job.

Carlos: What job **3 *will you* / *would you like*** to do?

Sam: I don't mind really. I just need money.

Carlos: Actually, my uncle **4 *will* / *might*** have some work for you.

Sam: Really?

Carlos: Yes, his new café **5 *will open* / *opens*** next Monday.

Sam: Wow. What jobs does he have?

Carlos: Well, I think he needs waiters.

Sam: I've never done that.

Carlos: That doesn't matter. He **6 *'ll* / *'s going to*** teach you.

Sam: I don't know…

Carlos: Well, I think I **7 *might go* / *'m going to*** see him tonight. I'll ask him about it.

Sam: Thank you. I **8 *will* / *'d*** really like to be a waiter.

Carlos: Cool.

Sam: You should ask him for a job, too. **9 *Wouldn't you like* / *Won't you*** to work there with me?

2 Label the jobs. Use the words in the box.

architect postman receptionist singer soldier teacher vet waiter

1

_____

2

_____

3

_____

4

_____

5

_____

6

_____

7

_____

8

_____

3 **Answer these questions in full sentences about your best friend or brother/sister.**
Practise saying these.

1 What job would he / she like to do in the future?

_____

_____

2 Where would he / she like to study?

_____

_____

3 Does he/ she want to stay at home? Why / not?

_____

_____

4 Would he / she like be a businessman or woman? Why / not?

_____

_____

5 Do you think he / she will study Chinese in the future?

_____

_____

6 Might he / she get a part-time job next year?

_____

_____

7 When does he / she finish school?

_____

_____

4 **Write a paragraph about your plans for when you are eighteen. Think about:**

- education
- holidays
- helping at home
- helping other people
- getting a job
- other sports and activities

_____

_____

_____

_____

_____

_____

_____

_____

9.1 We are all different

1 Put the conversation in the correct order.

1	**Man:**	Excuse me? Are you Ms Tennant?
☐	**Man:**	Oh no! What a shame. Shall I take you to your hotel?
☐	**Woman:**	Thank you. It's nice to meet you, Louis.
☐	**Woman:**	Not great! I couldn't sleep.
☐	**Man:**	How was your flight?
☐	**Man:**	I'm Louis. Welcome to Canada.
☐	**Woman:**	Yes, please! Thank you.
☐	**Woman:**	Yes, I am. What's your name?

2 Choose the best word to complete each sentence. Practise saying these.

1 Sara:	Hi Doug, how are you?
Doug:	Not great, Sara. I've lost my phone.
Sara:	Oh no: How *annoying / nice / kind*!

2 Woman:	Oh no! I've missed my train.
Man:	Why don't you take the number 54 bus? The bus stop is quite close.
Woman:	What a *pity / shame / good idea*! Thanks.
Man:	You're welcome.

3 Girl:	I'm home! Are Grandma and Granddad still here Mum?
Mum:	No, sorry Petal. They left half an hour ago.
Girl:	Oh what a *pity / good idea / time*!

3 Read the information about three teenagers and some school exchanges. Which school exchange should each person choose?

1 Hector wants to stay in a large family so that he can practise his English with lots of different people. He is friendly and funny. He also loves pets. ☐

2 June is very interested in culture and would like to visit museums and do some sightseeing. She would also like to go to the theatre, cinema and music concerts while she is on her exchange. ☐

3 Theo is studying for his exams and he wants to have a bedroom to himself so that he can study in the evenings and at the weekends. He would like to try lots of typical foods while he is on his exchange.  ☐

a
Come and stay with the Green family. Stay on your own floor in our house. You will have your own bedroom, bathroom with a bath and a shower, and small study. There is a big kitchen and living room where you can spend time with the family when you want to. Mr Green is a chef and has offered to teach the exchange student how to cook some typical meals.

b
The Walsh family lives in the centre of the city so there are lots of opportunities to go out and visit interesting places. There are some amazing plays and concerts on in the summer. Please note that the house is quite small and you must share a room. There is no garden but they do live near a large city park.

c
With two parents, six children, one grandma and two cats and a bird, the Harper family house is never quiet and you won't be lonely on your school exchange. Please note that you will have to share a bedroom with your school exchange partner.

d
The Wang family would love to have a polite and sensible student come on a school exchange to spend time with their daughter Rebecca. They are a musical family and Rebecca plays the piano, clarinet and the violin. They would love to have a student who is also a musician come and stay.

4 **Write a description of a student who would enjoy doing an exchange with the extra family.**

_____

_____

_____

_____

5 **Rewrite these sentences using the modal passive.**

1 The school might cancel the school exchange.
   The school exchange might be cancelled.

2 The family might take you to the museum.

   _____

3 The cleaner should clean your room on Monday.

   _____

4 Someone should put the ice cream in the freezer.

   _____

5 Someone needs to feed the fish.

   _____

6 Umberto ought to take out the rubbish.

   _____

7 No one can fix the piano.

   _____

8 You mustn't wear these glasses – they're Grandpa's and are too strong for you.

   _____

9.2 Let's celebrate!

1 Label the photos with the words from the box.

church   decorations   fireworks   to hug   mosque   parade   present

1

_____

2

_____

3

_____

4

_____

5

_____

6

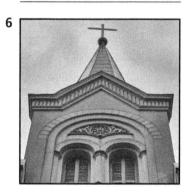

_____

2 Complete the sentences. Make nouns from the verbs in brackets.

1 My friend is a _____ with a band. **(sing)**

2 I can't find any _____ about the college online. **(inform)**

3 What's your favourite type of _____. **(entertain)**

4 The teachers put up lots of _____ in the school hall for the end of term party. **(decorate)**

5 Giles is a very good _____. **(ski)**

6 This is Mrs Guzman, she's my _____. **(employ)**

7 It's difficult to find _____ in our town now that the factory has closed. **(employ)**

8 I believe that every child should have a good _____. **(educate)**

9 Look! That's the man from the new shampoo _____. **(advertise)**

10 My aunt is a train _____. **(drive)**

7

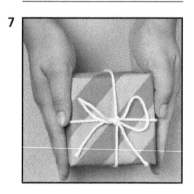

_____

3 **Read the text. Decide if sentences 1–10 are true (T), false (F) or not mentioned (NM).**

Mardi Gras is a famous festival in New Orleans, USA. It happens in the spring. There is a huge parade that goes through the streets of the city. People put on special clothes, which are purple, green and gold. It's very colourful. There are lots of music bands, so it's very loud. People have picnics and eat typical Cajun food, which is spicy. They also eat a special cake called King's cake. It has coloured sugar on the top in the special Mardi Gras colours purple, green and gold, and it has a special toy inside it.

1 A lot of people know about the Mardi Gras festival.	**T / F / NM**
2 It takes place in March.	**T / F / NM**
3 There are special Mardi Gras colours.	**T / F / NM**
4 The first Mardi Gras festival was in 1771.	**T / F / NM**
5 Cajun food does not have a strong taste.	**T / F / NM**
6 People go to their family's house after the parade to have a barbecue.	**T / F / NM**
7 Food is a very important part of the festival.	**T / F / NM**
8 King's cake is purple, green and orange.	**T / F / NM**
9 Mardi Gras is a quiet festival.	**T / F / NM**
10 Children like what is inside every King's cake.	**T / F / NM**

4 **Write a paragraph about your favourite festival. Use the questions to help you. Practise saying this paragraph.**

- What is the festival called and when is it?
- Why do you celebrate it?
- Who do you celebrate it with?
- What special food you eat at the festival?
- How do you celebrate it? (decorations, visiting family and friends …)
- Why do you like it?

_____
_____
_____
_____
_____
_____
_____

9.3 What we eat

1 Put the letters in the correct order to make food words.

1 shif nad pisch _____

2 oledib gegs _____

3 stoar nidenr _____

4 staap _____

5 abens _____

6 rucry _____

2 Look at the pictures that show what Lila ate on her school exchange. Write the correct letter for each sentence.

1 On Monday, Lila had dinner at a pizza restaurant with her exchange friend, Alice. ☐

2 Lila learned to make a roast dinner. ☐

3 Alice's parents made the girls do the washing up. ☐

4 Alice made Lila try some typical cheese. ☐

5 Alice promised to take Lila to eat fish and chips. ☐

3 Complete each sentence using the correct form of one of the verbs from the box.

ask help remind tell want

1 'Will you come to my birthday party?'

Fiona _____ me to come to her birthday party.

2 'Don't forget to send Grandma a birthday card.'

Mum _____ me to send Grandma a birthday card.

3 'You get the flour and I'll get the eggs.'

Anya _____ me to get the flour and eggs for the cake.

4 'Can you put the decorations up, please?'

Dad _____ me to put the decorations up.

5 'Don't sit there.'

The teacher _____ the students not to sit there.

4 **Choose the best words to complete the story.**

'Fady,' Assia said, 'you promised
1 _____ me to the parade today.' Assia was Fady's little sister. She was six. 'Oh no! Fady didn't want
2 _____ to the parade with Assia. He knew she wouldn't like it. 'Please!' she said.

'Are you sure you want to go?' Fady asked her.

'Yes, yes, yes,' Assia said. 'Help me to put on my best dress.'

At the parade, the dancers made Assia **3** _____, but the music was loud and it made her cry. So Fady offered **4** _____ her an ice cream. It was getting dark and Fady thought they should go home. But Assia wanted **5** _____ the fireworks.

'The fireworks will be very loud,' Fady told her. 'Let's go home.' Assia started **6** _____ and ran away from him. He ran after her. There were lots of people everywhere and he could not see her. It took Fady fifteen minutes to find his sister. Fady was angry. He decided **7** _____ the parade. He made Assia **8** _____ his hand all the way home.

'Did you have a nice time?' their parents asked them.

'No!' they both said together.

1 A take   **B** to take

2 A go   **B** to go

3 A smile   **B** to smile

4 A buy   **B** to buy

5 A see   **B** to see

6 A cry   **B** to cry

7 A leave   **B** to leave

8 A hold   **B** to hold

5 **Answer the questions about you. Write complete sentences. Practise saying these.**

1 What have you agreed to do this week?

_____

2 What films make you laugh?

_____

3 What jobs do your parents make you do at home?

_____

4 What have you learned to do recently?

_____

5 What food makes you feel sick?

_____

9.4 Globalization

1 Look at the information. Complete the text. Use the words from the box.

> a quarter   half   seven-eighths   two-thirds

Multinational companies in different business areas

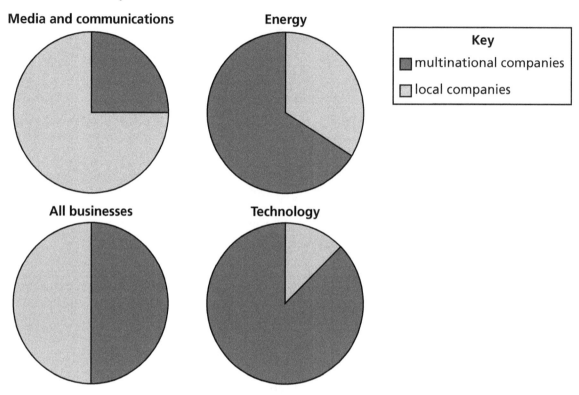

Media and communications

Energy

All businesses

Technology

Key
- ■ multinational companies
- ☐ local companies

> The Multinational companies are companies that have offices in many countries around the world. The number of multinational companies in the world is growing. We can see that
> **1** _____ of all businesses around the world are multinationals. In some areas local companies are doing quite well, for example in media and communications where multinationals are only **2** _____ of the companies. However, in other areas, such as energy, there are many more multinationals than local companies: Multinationals have **3** _____ of the business. The biggest area for multinationals is technology:
> **4** _____ of all technology companies are multinationals.

2 Underline the adverbs of degree in each sentence. One sentence has two adverbs of degree.

1 That was a good film. I found it quite exciting.
2 The company has exactly 15,000 employees.
3 Only very big multinational companies can set up a business in this city.
4 I'd really like to work for a multinational company.
5 They sell their products all around the world.
6 He's a very important businessman who is on TV all the time.

9.5 We are world citizens

1 Complete the crossword. Use the words from the box.

> citizen community
> ideas neighbours
> social media

Clues
Across

1 I was born in Scotland and I live in Wales. I am a British _____

2 I follow stories about what is happening in the world by looking at _____ on my phone.

4 All our friends and _____ came to the street festival.

Down

1 I live in a small _____ and everyone knows each other.

3 Young people are usually very open to new _____.

2 Match the halves of the verb phrases.

1 to go   **a** the news online
2 to understand another   **b** culture
3 to learn a   **c** people
4 to read   **d** language
5 to meet new   **e** travelling

3 Add a comma (,) to five of these sentences to make them correct.

1 If I went to India I'd see the Taj Mahal.
2 If I went to China I'd walk along the Great Wall.
3 I'd get a cat if I lived by myself.
4 If I lost my keys I'd tell my parents.
5 We'd catch the train if we left now.
6 My parents would be angry if I had my hair cut too short.
7 If my grandparents came to visit I'd bake them a cake.
8 If I lived by the sea I would swim every day.

4 Put the words in the correct order to make sentences.

1 for a run / If / wasn't / I / I / would / tired, / go

_____

2 exams, / have a party / passed / If / would / I / my / all / I

_____

3 car, / a / had / If / drive / learn / to / was / I / would / I

_____

4 hospital / I / would / go / If / broke / leg, / my / the / to

_____

5 new / I / If / would / buy / jeans/ some / I / mum / my / some / money, / gave / me

_____

5 Complete these sentences using the second conditional so they are true for you. Practise saying these.

1 If I didn't go to school, _____
2 If I went to London in the UK, _____
3 If my family moved to another country, _____
4 If a new student started at my school, _____
5 I'd talk to my headteacher _____
6 I'd buy my friend a present _____
7 I'd have more money _____
8 If I was hungry, _____

6 Write the questions for sentences 1–4 in activity 5.

1 *What would you do if you... ?* _____
2 _____
3 _____
4 _____

10.1 Technology and me

1 Look at the pictures. Put the letters in the correct order to make words.

1
micco

2
omrf

3
tooneokb

4
trelet

5
tone

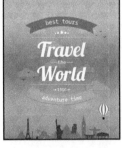

6
gizaanme

7
spewnapre

8
okob

9
rorecbhu

10
factteercii

11
cleatir

12
lilb

2 Match the sentence halves.

1 This service is not free of charge – you

2 I really love wearing this shirt because

3 My electric bike is so fast

4 The temperature is very

5 The maths exam was very hard so

6 You can borrow my headphones but please

7 I wouldn't spend £800 just on a phone,

8 In my country it rains a lot and

a I didn't answer all the questions.

b I think it's silly.

c it's normal to take an umbrella everywhere you go.

d have to pay for it.

e high today – almost 38 degrees.

f be careful with them!

g it's very comfortable.

h that sometimes it's quicker than driving.

3 Look at the table about the habits of four students.
Then complete the sentences with the correct name.

1 _____ almost always makes notes at school.

2 _____ almost never reads articles
for schoolwork.

3 _____ almost never writes a letter
every week.

4 _____ rarely reads a book at bedtime.

5 _____ almost always messages grandparents.

6 _____ almost never messages grandparents.

Mohammed   Claire

Rikki   Candy

ACTIVITY	Monday	Tuesday	Wednesday	Thursday	Friday
Make notes at school	Mohammed ✓ Rikki ✗	Mohammed ✓ Rikki ✗	Mohammed ✓ Rikki ✓	Mohammed ✓ Rikki ✓	Mohammed ✗ Rikki ✓
Read an article for schoolwork	Claire ✓ Candy ✓	Claire ✓ Candy ✗	Claire ✓ Candy ✗	Claire ✓ Candy ✗	Claire ✗ Candy ✗
Write a letter every week	Mohammed ✗ Claire ✗	Mohammed ✗ Claire ✗	Mohammed ✗ Claire ✗	Mohammed ✗ Claire ✗	Mohammed ✗ Claire ✓
Read a book at bedtime	Candy ✗ Rikki ✓	Candy ✓ Rikki ✓	Candy ✗ Rikki ✓	Candy ✗ Rikki ✗	Candy ✗ Rikki ✓
Message grandparents	Mohammed ✗ Claire ✓	Mohammed ✗ Claire ✓	Mohammed ✗ Claire ✓	Mohammed ✗ Claire ✓	Mohammed ✗ Claire ✗

4 Complete the text with the correct word from the box.

> broken latest old-fashioned technology telephone tiring typing

My friend John doesn't really like
1 _____ on the computer. He prefers
2 _____ things like writing in a
notebook. Maybe it's because his mum
and dad don't like technology much either.
For example, they have a 3 _____
instead of mobile phones.

He did have a mobile phone a few years
ago. However I think it's 4 _____ now.
He says using technology, like looking at a
screen for a long time, is really 5 _____
for his eyes. I'm completely different. I love all kinds of 6 _____. I love having the
7 _____ model of my mobile phone and tablet.

5 **Write tag questions for these sentences.** EXTENSION

1 This is an interesting video, _____?

2 Gregor's not into downloading audiobooks, _____?

3 They didn't text you, _____?

4 You need a new mobile phone, _____?

5 Looking at social media late at night isn't good for you, _____?

6 A new phone is expensive, _____?

6 **Read the conversation and decide if the statements are true (T) or false (F).**

1 Stefan needs help with his homework.   T/F

2 Stefan wants to ask Freya about how she uses social media.   T/F

3 She prefers audiobooks.   T/F

4 She hasn't written a letter for a long time.   T/F

5 They disagree about writing and receiving letters.   T/F

Stefan: Hi, Freya! Can I ask you some questions for my school project? It's about how you use technology.

Freya: Yes, sure – but I've only got a few minutes.

Stefan: Great, it won't take long…

Freya: OK. What's the first question?

Stefan: Do you prefer reading a book or listening to an audio book?

Freya: Actually, I really don't like listening to books online. I much prefer holding a book in my hands.

Stefan: Thanks! And here is the second question. When was the last time you wrote a letter?

Freya: Last week we wrote a letter to a pen friend in another country in our English lesson. I quite enjoyed writing it.

Stefan: It's a bit strange writing a letter, isn't it? Why not just write an email?

Freya: But it's fun to get a letter in the post, isn't it?

Stefan: I never receive any so really, I don't see the point.

Freya: Well, I think it's fun.

Stefan: Thanks for answering my questions, Freya!

10.2 Life then and now

1 Choose the correct words to complete the sentences.

1 Many years ago people *used / use* to drive ride horses not cars.

2 Did you *use / used* to have a toy train when you were a child?

3 Yes, I *use / used* to have a toy train.

4 *Did / Do* your parents *use / used* to have mobile phones when they were young?

5 No, they *didn't use / not used* to have any kind of phone.

6 Did your grandmother *used to have / use to* have Wi-Fi in her house when she was young?

7 No, there *didn't use to be / not use to be* any internet when she was born.

2 Put the words in the correct order to make sentences.

1 Sasha / old / about / eighteen / is / years

_____

2 arrive / to / London / we / are / in / about / ?

_____

3 a / different / phone / make / about / call / a / I'm / to / . / you / Could / work / in / room?

_____

4 Don't / teacher / worry! / to / tell / is / us / answers / the / about / the / .

_____

5 Look! / it / is / snow / about / to / think / I

_____

3 Choose the correct option in each sentence to complete the conversation.

A: *Did / Have* you ever bought a mobile phone?

B: Yes, I *have / did*.

A: How many phones *did you have / have you had* in your life?

B: I can't remember! *I had / 've had* so many.

A: When *have you bought / did you buy* your first phone?

B: I *bought / have bought* my first mobile phone three years ago. It *was / has been* blue.

A: Where *have / did* you get it?

B: My parents have *bought / bought* it online.

A: How much *has / did* it cost?

B: It *cost / has cost* 200 euros.

4 Answer A's questions in activity 3 so that they are true for you. Practise saying these sentences.

5 Complete the text with the correct version of the verbs in brackets.

Travel **1** _____ (change) so much since the beginning of the 1900s because there **2** _____ (be) so much new technology. Most of our great-grandparents **3** _____ (not have) cars. Instead, they use to **4** _____ (walk) to most places. To go to different cities, they travelled by bus or train. However, in the 1920s and 30s more people **5** _____ (start) to buy cars and the age of driving began.

6 Now read the next part of the text and choose the correct option.

During the second half of the 20th century, more and more people **1** *flew / fly* by aeroplane and **2** *travel / travelled* to different countries on holiday. By the 1970s, flying by plane **3** *had become / has become* much faster and easier. People could even **4** *fly / flew* much further to places like Australia. It only **5** *takes / is taking* about 24 hours to get there – that's more than 15,000 kilometres from London. Now, planes **6** *can / could* carry more people and travel for longer without stopping.

7 Write a paragraph about how life and technology has changed since your great grandparents were young. Use the photos and notes to help you.

Before
streets quieter… few cars …. horses not cars … no internet…
writing letters, go to shops
Now:
electric cars, Wi-Fi, mobile phones, fast internet, online shopping

Then and Now

_____
_____
_____
_____
_____
_____

10.3 Technology in the home

1 Write questions for these answers.

1 _____

I've had my phone for three years.

2 _____

I bought my phone three years ago.

3 _____

I bought my phone online.

4 _____

No, nobody bought me this phone as a present. I bought it myself.

5 _____

No, I've never dropped my phone.

6 _____

No, I never use my phone to write emails.

7 _____

Yes, I would really like a new phone.

8 _____

I think I'll get a new phone next year.

2 Read and complete the text with a word from the box.

going   won't   take   takes   will

At the moment it **1** _____ many hours to put energy into an electric car. But in the future, it will probably only **2** _____ a few minutes! A lot of people think that in the future, we **3** _____ drive cars anymore. Instead, they say that we will have intelligent cars which **4** _____ drive themselves. Is this really **5** _____ to happen? What do you think?

3 **Write the words from the box in the correct places.**

armchair carpet light mirror shampoo shelf
sink sofa tap toilet toothbrush towel

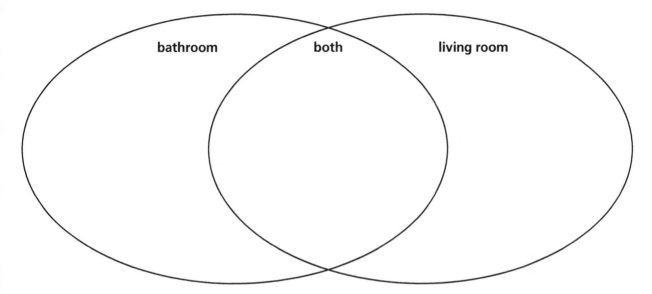

bathroom   both   living room

5 **Read the text about intelligent homes and decide if the statements are true (T) or false (F).**

Hi! So there are several reasons why I don't think we will all have intelligent homes in the future. Firstly, not everyone can afford an intelligent home. It would be very expensive and difficult to change all the devices in every house. Secondly, people might be happy with their home. They may not want to change it. For example, my parents love their home and they told me they don't want to have an intelligent home.

Finally, some people say it is not private to have an intelligent home. You have to share a password with a company so that you can turn on your lights. So, I don't think I will have an intelligent home in the future. But I do think that intelligent homes are more comfortable than normal homes because you don't ever have to get up from your sofa!

1 The writer thinks that it's easy to change a normal home into an intelligent home. **T/F**
2 The writer says that some people don't want to change the technology in their home. **T/F**
3 The writer says an intelligent home is controlled by a company. **T/F**
4 The writer would like an intelligent home in the future. **T/F**
5 The writer thinks that normal homes are not as comfortable. **T/F**

10.4 Technology in the future

1 Read the text and complete the gaps in the text with: *also, instead, and, or*. You will use some words more than once.

I think that in the future I'll work in business. I don't know where I will work. It might be in my own country **1** _____ I might work in a different country. I would quite like to work in London. I would **2** _____ quite like to work in New York. However, if I can't work in business, then I would like to do something creative **3** _____. So, I'm going to study business and **4** _____ a creative subjects, like design technology **5** _____ art at university. I have an older sister and an older brother **6** _____ they work in business so I want to do the same thing!

2 Complete the sentences about the future with your opinions. Give a reason or add more information to each sentence. Practise saying these sentences.

1 People *will / won't* fly in planes _____

_____

2 Cities *will / won't* look very different _____

_____

3 We *will / won't* the same food as now _____

_____

4 Education *will / won't* only be online _____

_____

5 Everyone *will / won't* work from home and not go to an office _____

_____

6 There *will / won't* be cars in cities _____

_____

7 Clothes *will / won't* look very different _____

_____

8 Our homes *will / won't* be smaller _____

_____

10.5 New worlds

1 Read the article and complete the gaps with the correct words from the box. You will need to use some words more than once.

> been   had   have   know   saw   use   was

Did you **1** _____ that many devices that we **2** _____ today were first invented in comics and films in the past! Look at that intelligent watch on your arm – people first **3** _____ something like this in a comic called *Dick Tracy* in 1946! A lot of other technology that had only **4** _____ in the dreams of comic book artists and writers, are now part of modern life. For example, we **5** _____ used video chats and smart phones for a long time. In a 1960s television show called *The Six Million Dollar Man* there **6** _____ a man with robot arms and legs. Now doctors can make these for people who have **7** _____ an accident and lost an arm or leg. Children first **8** _____ small flying objects that carried cameras on them in *Batman* comics in 1957 and modern children now **9** _____ them as toys! We call them 'drones'. What other devices from comics will we **10** _____ in the future?

2 Look at the photos and find them in the article. Write a sentence about each device under the photos.

a drone

A drone is a small flying object that sometimes carries a camera on it.

an intelligent watch

_____

_____

_____

a robot arm

_____

_____

_____

a smart phone

_____

_____

_____

a video chat

_____

_____

_____

3 Read the text and choose the correct tense of the verbs.

Elon Musk **1** *started / had started* a company called X.com when he **2** *had been / was* 28 years old.
He **3** *has / had* already sold a video game to a computer company when he **4** *was / had been* 12 years old.

As a child, he **5** *had / has* dreamed of using technology to have adventures. He **6** *read / has read* a lot of comics like *Iron Man*. In the comics he **7** *has / had* seen flying cars and so he **8** *wanted / has wanted* to build them himself. Do you think he will make his dream come true?

4 Write full sentence answers to these questions.

1 What would you like to study at university? Why?

_____

2 What would you do if you lost your phone?

_____

3 What things do you need to do to stay healthy?

_____

4 What's more comfortable: travelling by plane or train? Why?

_____

5 What time does your first class start on a Monday?

_____

6 What have you done today?

_____

7 What is the best thing you have done recently?

_____

8 Have you ever been to another country?

_____

9 What have you just done?

_____

10 Have you ever ridden a motorbike?

_____

11 What do you want to do in the summer?

_____

12 What do you think you'll do tonight?

_____

13 What are you going to do tomorrow?

_____

14 What makes you laugh?

_____